Fredericksburg, Texas

150 Years of Paintings and Drawings

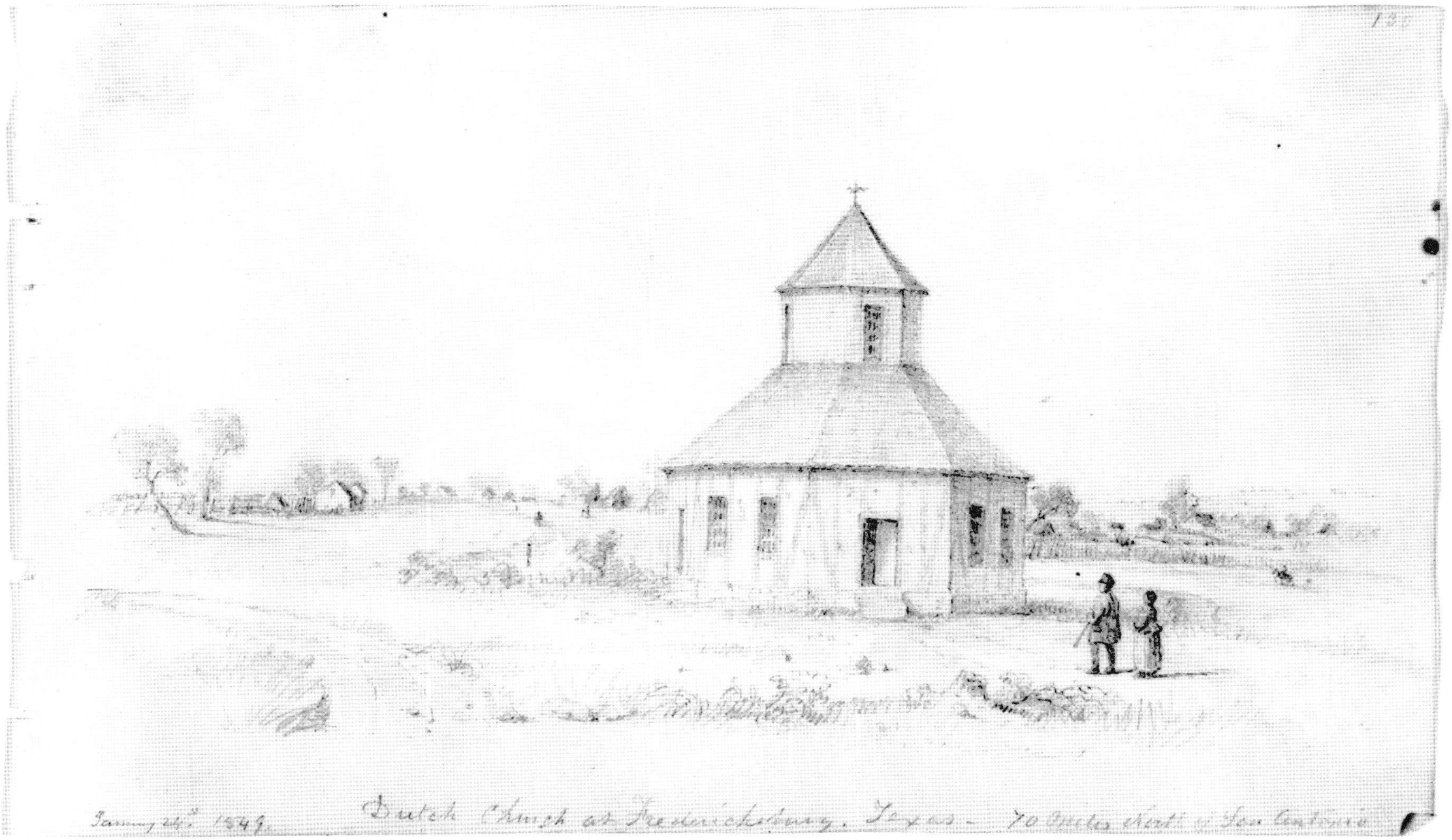

Text by Jack Maguire
Published by
Fredericksburg 150th Anniversary, Inc.
Book design and production by
Burdett & Associates • Fredericksburg, Texas

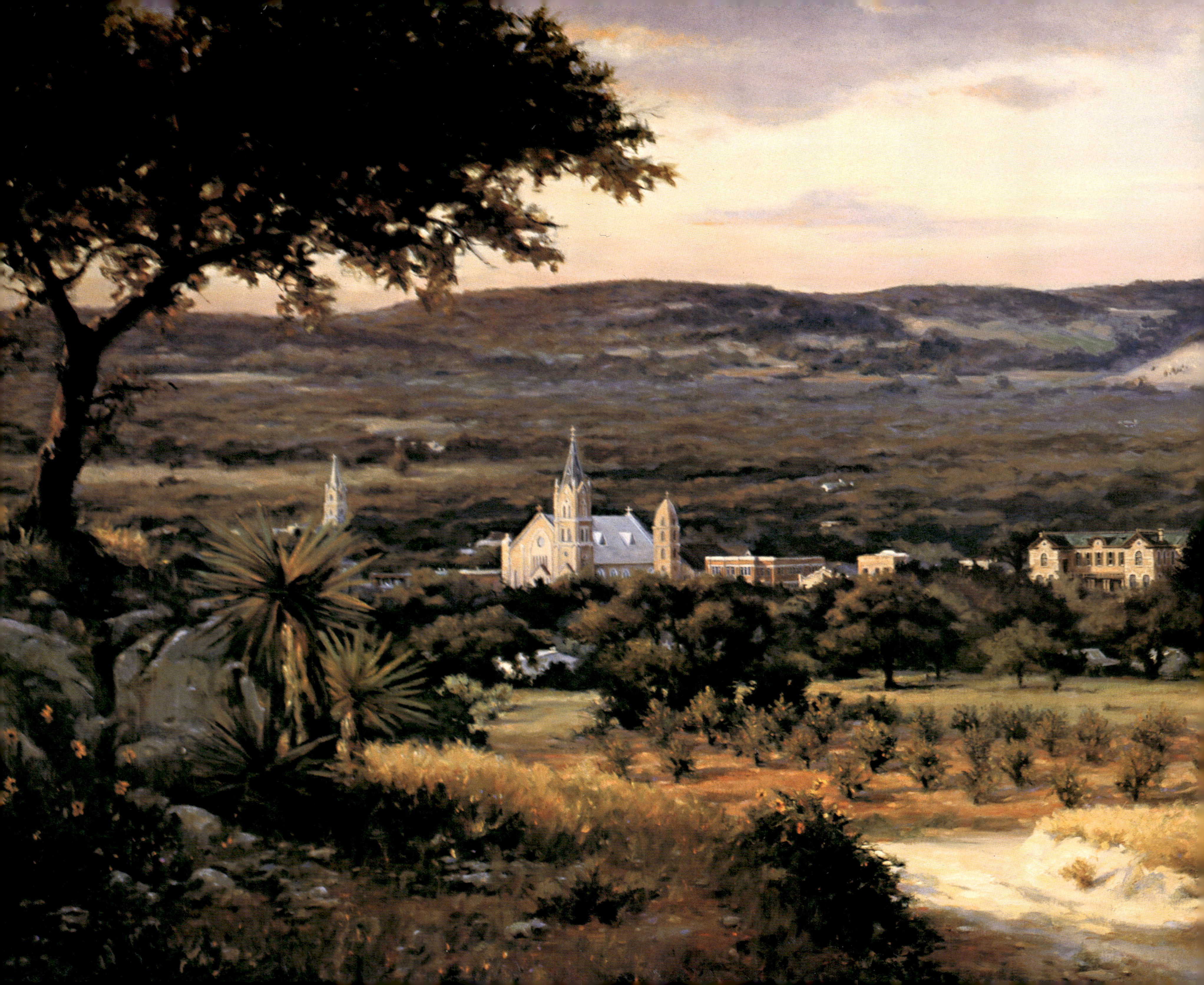

Fredericksburg

TEXAS

150 Years of Paintings and Drawings

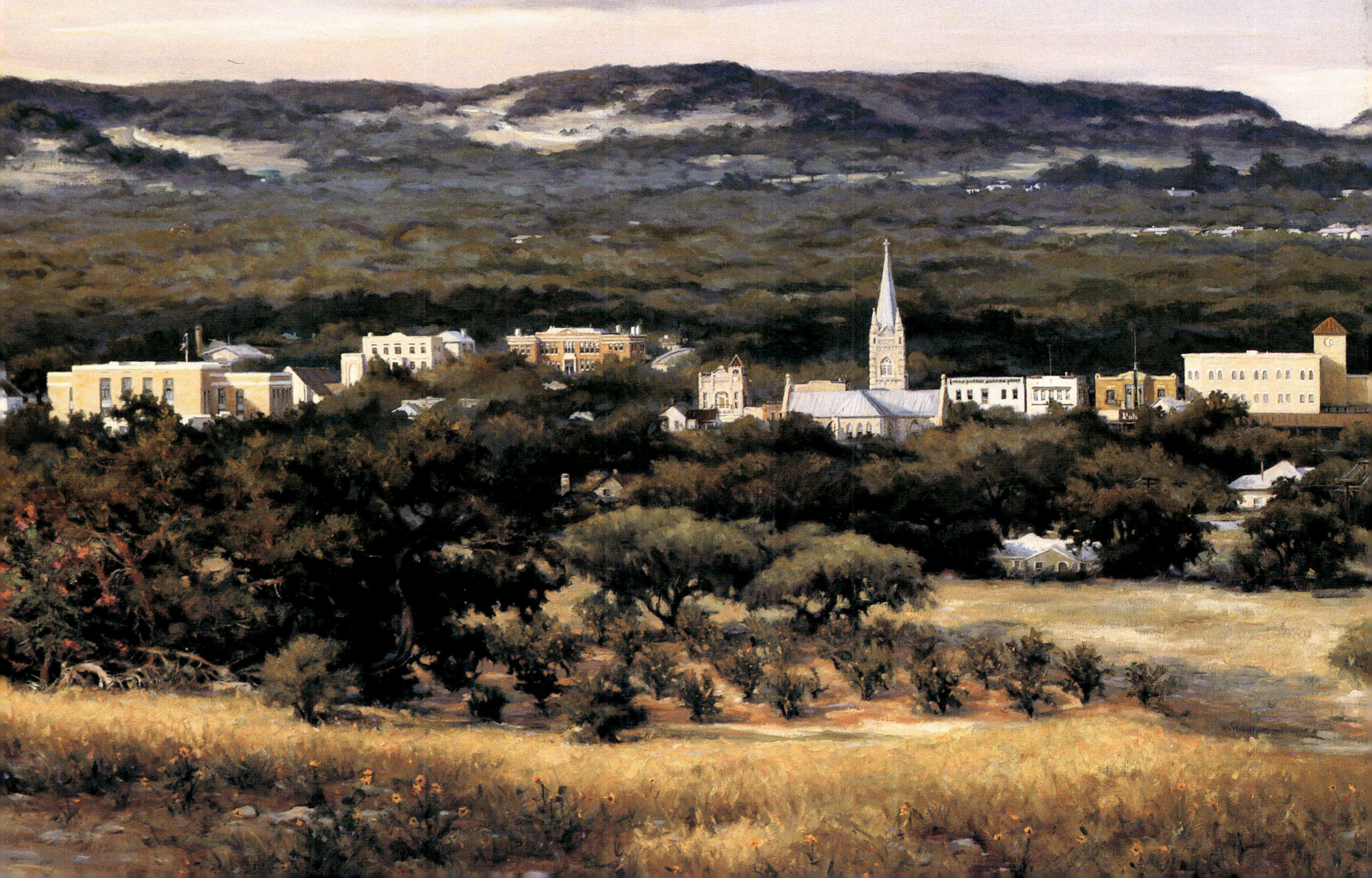

Published and Distributed by
Fredericksburg 150th Anniversary, Inc.
P.O. Box 111, Dept. 150
126 W. Main
Fredericksburg, Texas 78624
210-997-7521 (fax 210-997-1861)

ISBN #0-9648036-0-7
Library of Congress Catalog Card #95-70460
First Edition

Text by Jack Maguire
Edited by Ann Maguire
Book Design by William H. Burdett, Dean A. Heep and Mark Haworth at Burdett & Associates • Fredericksburg,Texas
Digital Assembly by Dean A. Heep and William H. Burdett
Project Photography by Joe Beckendorf
Research by Janice Langerhans (chair), Betty Ethel, Nancy Hardison, Ruby Lee Clark and Mark Haworth
Printed and Bound in Hong Kong

COVER AND TITLE PAGE 2 AND 3
"FREDERICKSBURG-AN ENDURING HERITAGE"
BY MARK HAWORTH
3' X 12' OIL ON CANVAS
From the Collection of Bank One Texas NA

TITLE PAGE 1
"DUTCH CHURCH AT FREDERICKSBURG, TEXAS-
70 MILES NORTH OF SAN ANTONIO, JANUARY 24, 1849"
BY SETH EASTMAN
From the Collection of McNay Art Museum,
San Antonio, Texas
Gift of the Pearl Brewing Company

COPYRIGHT PAGE
"TEXAS LONGHORN"
PENCIL SKETCH BY CHARLES BECKENDORF
Courtesy of Charles Beckendorf Gallery

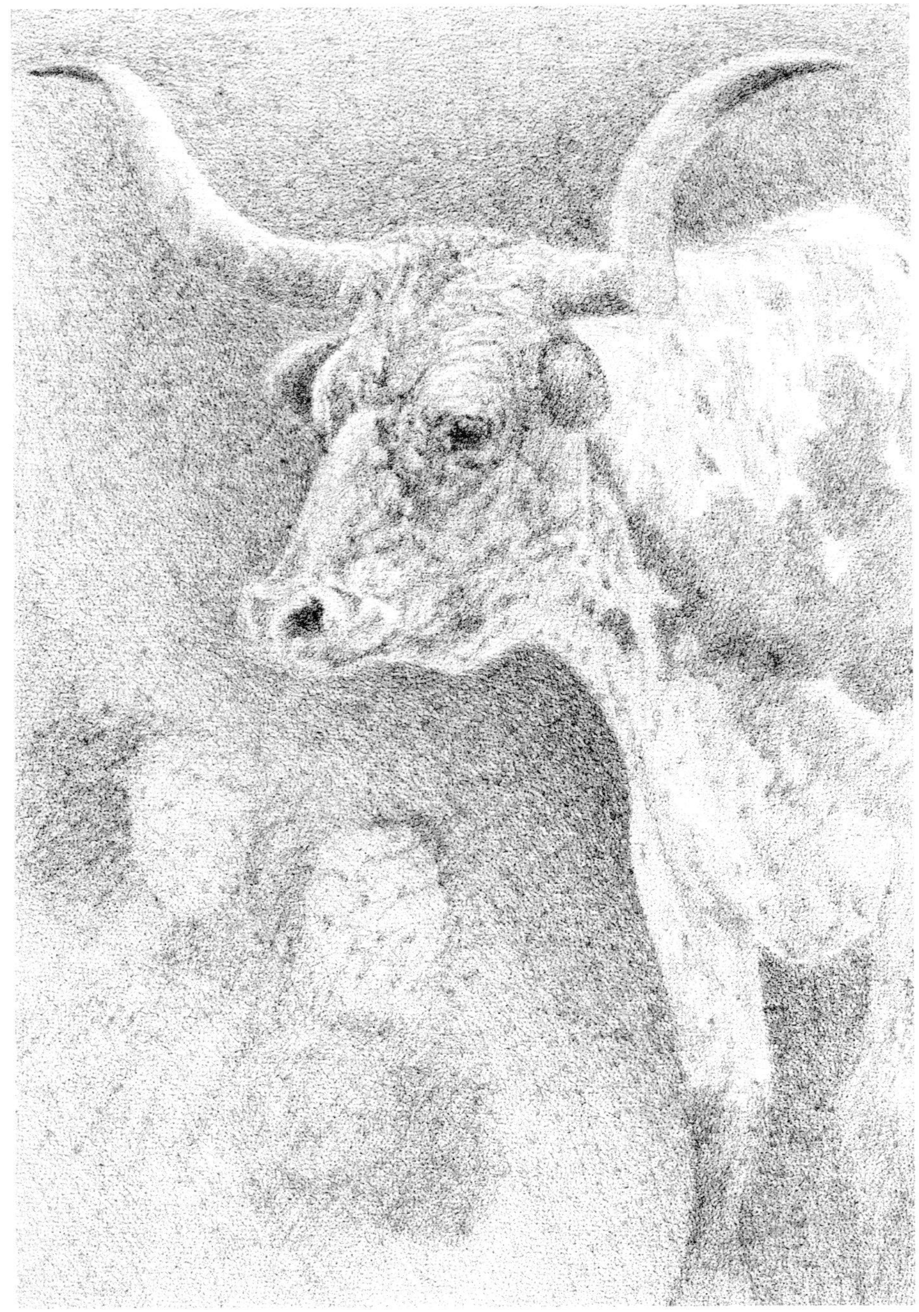

Contents

Letter from the 150th Anniversary Committee 6

Author's Acknowledgements 7

Fredericksburg, Texas - The First 150 Years 8

Architecture is Art, Too 11

Folk Art 13

Artisans Today 14

It's May Day Every Day 15

The Limners 16

The Coming of the Professionals 17

The Sound of Music 18

Where the Arts are at Home 20

Biographies

Seth Eastman 1808-1875 24

Hermann Lungkwitz 1813-1891 29

Father Peter Tarrillion 1821-1900 33

Friedrich Richard Petri 1824-1857 35

Edward G. Eisenlohr 1872-1961 39

Harold Osman Kelly (Kelly Blue) 1884-1955 43

Felix Weinheimer 1885-1955 47

Edwina Mintel 1896-1966 49

Norbert Czarnowski 1897-1994 51

Lyne K. Lewis Harper 1897- 54

Edward Muegge (Buck) Schiwetz 1898-1984 57

Dollie Spidel Nabinger 1905-1988
and Virginia Muller 1930-1981 61

Edna Helen Bierschwale 1907-1975 65

Werner E. Weber 1909-1974 67

Gotthold G. Lentz 1912- 70

John D. McClusky 1914-1994 72

Elsa Muranyi Ingels 1916- 76

Onieta Merrie Bartholmae 1918-1982 79

Jack Cupper 1920- 82

Irene Klein 1921- 86

Lee Ethel 1926-1992 90

Charles Beckendorf 1930- 94

G. Harvey 1933- 98

John Austin Hanna 1942- 102

Mark Haworth 1952- 106

FREDERICKSBURG 150TH ANNIVERSARY

Founded May 8, 1846

1846-1996

May 3 - 12 1996

150TH COMMITTEE

JIMMY ALEXANDER
W 997-7521 or 997-7952
CATHY COLLIER
W 997-2155 or 997-4837
CONNIE CRENWELGE
W 997-9865 or 997-3670
REV. ROBERT DEMING
997-6251
PEGGY DODDS
W 997-9865 or 997-3623
TIM DOOLEY
W 997-2118 or 997-7345
SHERMAN D. DURST
W 997-6531 or 997-5255
LESTER FRANTZEN
W 997-9531 or 997-4985
JAN FRITZ
W 997-2197 or 997-5909
DEBBIE FARQUHAR-GARNER
W 997-8515 or 997-0374
BARBARA HEINEN
W 997-7421 or 997-5682
LAURIE JENSCHKE
W 997-2288 or 997-8263
MARTY KADERLI
W 997-8600 or 997-7367
JOE KAMMLAH
W 997-6523 or 997-6289
KENN KNOPP
997-7273
TIM KOOCK
W 997-9554 or 997-9728
FRITZ METZGER
W 997-2251 or 997-2867
KAREN OESTREICH
W 997-9591 or 997-2554
TROY OTTMERS
W 997-2240 or 997-8277
HECTOR PEDREGON
W 997-9527 or 997-5090
PENNY C. REEH
W 997-6523 or 997-6068
W.A. (BILLY) ROEDER
W 997-7502 or 997-5962
LORETTA SCHMIDT
997-3234

FREDERICKSBURG, TEXAS - 150 Years of Paintings and Drawings will become a fine addition to the history of a community such as ours that is steeped in preserving its heritage at every turn.

Each twenty-fifth anniversary since its founding Fredericksburg has found cause to celebrate. At each celebration the community took time to look back and reflect on the hardships of those first settlers and those early years. Throughout our first 150 years there have been several permanent and lasting tributes to our history and the pioneers who faced many diversities to settle here. This book will continue that heritage as it brings to life a facet of our community that has brought enjoyment to all from the early founding days through today.

This book is a first step to help preserve the heritage of the many painters and fellow artists of our community. They have never been so honored as a group and many have not even been honored so graciously individually.

Fredericksburg and Gillespie County had and have many fine artisans, which makes it very difficult to showcase everyone. The selections here are a good representation of the many artists past, present and future that we and the world have enjoyed. The selection process to deliver this work involved many hours, that stretched into days that became weeks and then months.

The 150th Anniversary Committee would like to thank all of those who were involved with this work for their hours were many and their rewards were few except in the fact of knowing that they will have left another enduring mark in the long and wonderful heritage of our community.

FREDERICKSBURG, TEXAS - 150 Years of Paintings and Drawings will become one of the landmarks in our history along with the other dedications that will be made at the 150th celebration May 3-12, 1996.

Sherman D. Durst, President
150th Anniversary of Fredericksburg, Inc.

FREDERICKSBURG 150TH ANNIVERSARY, INC. • P.O. BOX 111, DEPARTMENT 150 • 126 WEST MAIN
FREDERICKSBURG, TX 78624 • 210-997-7521 • (FAX 997-1861)

Author's Acknowledgments

by Jack Maguire

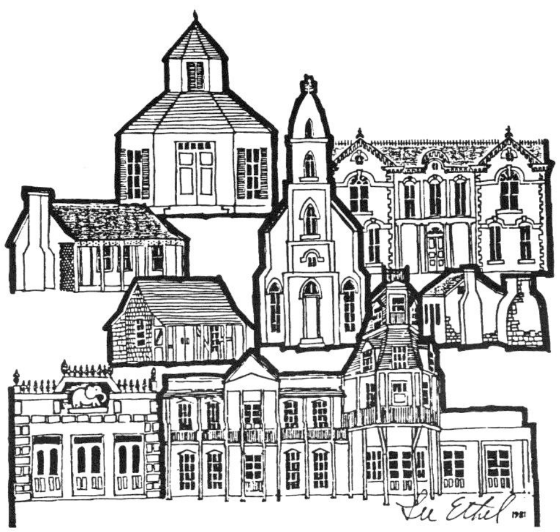

DRAWING BY LEE ETHEL
Courtesy of Betty Ethel

Unlike most books, this one is the work of a Committee.

In planning 12 months of celebrating the city's century and a half of existence, a group of progressive, but heritage conscious, citizens formed Fredericksburg 150th Anniversary, Inc. to plan a series of events celebrating this birthday in 1996.

It is appropriate that these include an exhibition of the works of selected local artists, past and present, and the publication of a book briefly profiling their lives.

To accomplish this, an Art Book Committee was formed. Members include active artists, the widow of a prominent artist, a public school teacher of art and some who are long-time supporters of the arts. The committee was organized with Janice Langerhans as chair. Members included Betty Ethel, Nancy Hardison, Ruby Lee Clark, Billy Burdett and Mark Haworth.

It was the Committee's assignment to select the artists that are showcased in both the exhibit and the book---a difficult task since literally hundreds of artists, part-time hobbyists and full-time professionals, have called Fredericksburg home over the last 150 years. Once the Committee made its selections, each member was assigned to research the backgrounds of several of those to be included. This required many hours of interviewing living artists and the relatives of those who are deceased, plus checking libraries, art collections and other sources.

As the writer, my only assignment was to take their material and turn it into a book which those wanting more information about Fredericksburg's history as an art center would find interesting.

As anticipated, these volunteer researchers gave it their best, and I am eternally grateful.

We also were fortunate to have Billy Burdett, an experienced book designer, for his expertise in laying out and overseeing the printing and production of the book.

Lastly, I owe a debt of gratitude to my wife, Ann, my long-time editor and critic. In suggesting ideas and in revising and improving my work, she spent as many long hours as I did in bringing this manuscript to fruition.

Researching and writing a work of this kind was a new experience for each of us. However, like the pioneers who came to God's hills and settled Fredericksburg in 1846, it has been an experience we shall treasure always.

Jack Maguire

INTRODUCTION

Fredericksburg, Texas
The First 150 Years

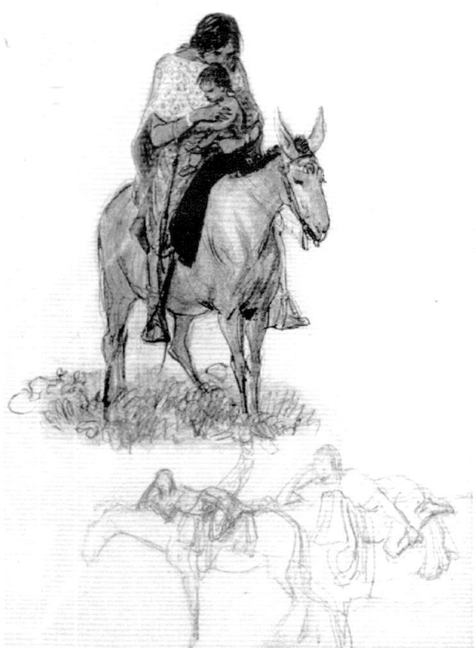

"WOMAN AND CHILD ON MULEBACK AND SKETCHES OF WOMAN ON HORSE" BY FRIEDRICH RICHARD PETRI
Courtesy of the Texas Memorial Museum Acc. #2269-3-1

Art has been integral to the Fredericksburg tradition since the arrival of the first 120 settlers from Germany on May 8, 1846. In a sense, the town owes its founding---at least, in part---to a form of the arts known as the novel.

It was a book with the unexciting title of *The Cabin Boy*. Its author was Karl Anton Posti who, like many of these eventual newcomers to Fredericksburg, had longed to leave a Europe that was facing economic and political chaos. Posti's dream came true when, as a young postulant in a German monastery, he abandoned his vows and fled to Texas.

To Posti, his new home was truly the Promised Land. Here he changed his name to "Charles Sealsfield" and wrote the novel, a kind of travel log, that would become a best seller in Europe. He filled his book with hyperbole, describing Texas as "a boundless field of green," the nearest thing to the garden of Eden. German readers loved it.

Many of his countrymen had not waited for Sealsfield's inspiration to send them to the United States on the first available boat. There already were dozens of German settlements in New York, the Middle west and Texas. In fact, with or without the influence of Sealsfield's book, Texas owes much of its development to German settlers.

It's true that the Spanish got here first. In 1519, Alonzo Alvarez de Piñeda was commissioned to map the Gulf coast for Spain and stopped off at Galveston Island. He claimed for Spain what now is Texas. In 1528, the Spanish explorer, Cabéza de Vaca, arrived and was shipwrecked near Galveston. However, it was two centuries before the Spanish established control over the region.

They did send some Catholic padres to erect a few missions and to begin Christianizing the Indians. They also built a presidio at San Antonio de Bexar, some 75 miles from the present Fredericksburg. But it was not until 1731 that the first settlers---the Canary Islanders---were sent to colonize near the Bexar presidio.

Even this action was taken, not because of Spain's interest in developing the area, but because the French had established a presence in Louisiana. Spain was concerned that this enemy nation might also decide to move into Texas.

After the Canary Islanders had established the first municipality in Texas, it was almost another century before Stephen F. Austin brought his Anglo colony of 300 to settle in Texas in 1821. The first Germans began to arrive a decade later. It was not until publication of *The Cabin Boy* and the promotional activities of a group of wealthy German aristocrats, however, that Texas became a magnet attracting thousands of their countrymen.

Whether the final destination in America was Texas or some other state, their decision to leave Germany was not an easy one. It meant leaving friends, home and sometimes close family members. To many it also meant deserting a life of culture that was unknown at that time in Texas. Although Sealsfield's book described Texas as "God's world immaculate," it would be years before this frontier state would provide some of the cultural niceties that were a part of daily life in Germany.

Among those who had read Sealsfield's glowing story of Texas were five sovereign princes and 16 noblemen. Although they probably questioned the veracity of some of the author's Texas brags, they also saw an opportunity to make some money while helping their countrymen achieve their goals of immigrating to the United States.

The group had an organization, *Mainzer Adelsverein* (Society of Noblemen). They met in 1842 at Bierbach on the Rhine near Mainz and formed the Society for the Protection of German Immigrants to Texas. Although they had learned much about Texas from Sealsfield's book and other publications that followed its popularity, they really knew very little about what prospective colonists could expect. From the start, the project was poorly organized and under financed.

That it succeeded at all is a tribute to the quality of those who accepted the challenge and decided to immigrate. As one writer described them:

"No higher class of citizenship ever immigrated to any country. Most were distressfully poor in money, but they were rich in brains and brawn, rich in energy and the highest purposes and noblest impulses. Out of this immigration, Texas received many of its greatest educators, physicians, mechanics, musicians writers and artists."

Responsibility for enrolling these people, transporting them to Texas and getting them settled in their new lives was assigned to a member of German royalty. The Society selected Carl, Prince of Solms, Lord of Braunfels, Grafenstein, Munzenberg, Wildenfels and Sonnenwalde, as Commissioner of the project. In 1845, he would lead the Society's first immigrants to Texas.

After a lengthy and turbulent ocean voyage, Prince Carl landed his charges at Indianola (dubbed Karlshaven by the Germans in his honor). They walked the long trail north to the Comal River where they established New Braunfels, the first settlement of the *Adelsverein* in Texas.

Meanwhile another aristocrat who was particularly attracted by the *Adelsverein* plan was Baron Ottfried Hans von Meusebach, the son of one of Germany's oldest and most prestigious families and the future founder of Fredericksburg. He had a superb education, having studied mining, the natural sciences, law, government, economics and banking. Also he was a patron of the arts.

The von Meusebachs moved in the best social circles. Among his friends were some of the nation's best known writers, painters and intellectuals. These included military leaders, teachers, the brothers Grimm (of fairy tale fame) and

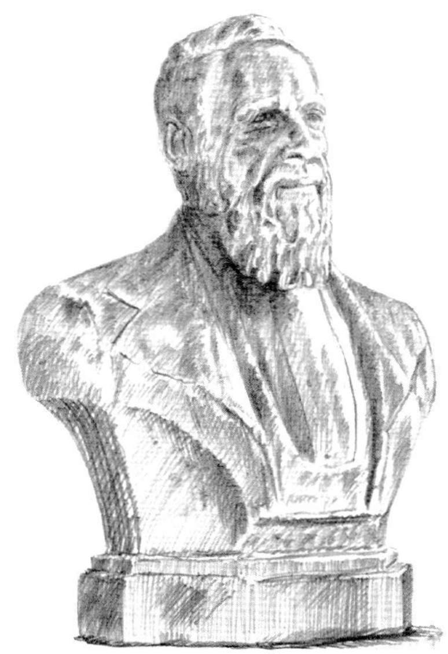

BRONZE BUST OF JOHN O. MEUSEBACH AT MARKTPLATZ
PENCIL DRAWING BY CHARLES BECKENDORF
Courtesy of Charles Beckendorf Gallery

others. Johan Wolfgang von Goethe, the great German poet, was a friend of the family until his death.

Although Meusebach found life in Germany both satisfying and exciting, his attraction to science helped to focus his interest on new discoveries. He had become intrigued with Sealsfield's book, possibly because the author pictured Texas as still savage, though exotic. In 1844, he wrote Count Carl Castell, head of the *Adelsverein*:

"I have been considering going to America to obtain a large enough property to be the basis of nature study and the furtherance thereof in those rich fields. I have had my eyes especially on Texas."

His opportunity to act came sooner than expected. After the problems of bringing the first group of settlers and establishing New Braunfels, Prince Carl stepped down as Commissioner. Meusebach took over.

Because of his background as an intellectual, Meusebach seems the least likely person to lead a group of immigrants to new homes on the frontier. One thing was certain, however. If he did so, he would bring the arts and culture of his native country with him.

The group headed by Meusebach was not unlike those that had come before. They brought little with them except their clothing, their tools and their skills. Many were well educated---some were from noble families---and they came from a society that had broad cultural interests. They also were blessed with that innate sense of beauty characteristic of the Germans. With this background, they would create a kind of "native" art not seen in Texas before.

Art, however, has also been described as "a learning experience," and these immigrants from a sophisticated country like Germany had much to learn about the frontier they had come to conquer. The "art" of living in a new and vastly different land was Lesson One.

Whatever their social status may or may not have been at home, in America there were no visible classes. This was a lesson Meusebach taught the settlers he brought to found Fredericksburg. Although he had named the town for royalty---Prince Friedrich Wilhelm Ludwig of the Prussian House of Hohenzollern and the highest ranking member of the *Adelsverein*---Meusebach dropped his own title and first names. He became simply John O. Meusebach and remained so until his death.

None of the newcomers to Friedrichsburg (the official name until changed years later by postal authorities) were concerned about social status. They were too busy building homes, cultivating crops, adjusting to the mores of a new environment and providing for the necessities of everyday living. Neither was there opportunity for their natural artistic talents to appear. However, their love of beauty and their sense of good design---two major attributes of fine art---were apparent in the early structures they built, many of which still stand.

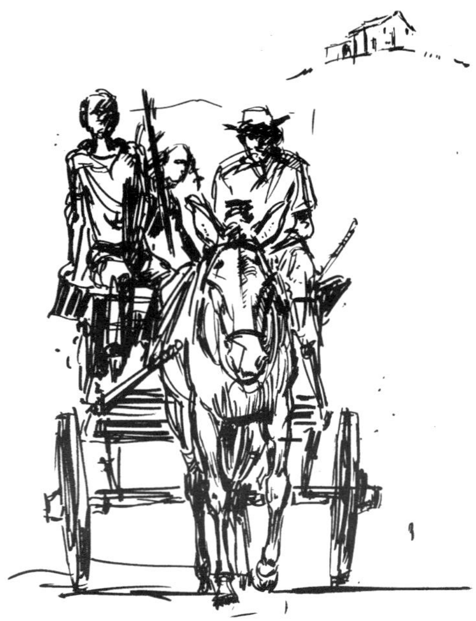

MULE AND CART STUDY
BY JOHN AUSTIN HANNA
Courtesy of John and Sherrie Hanna

Architecture is Art, too

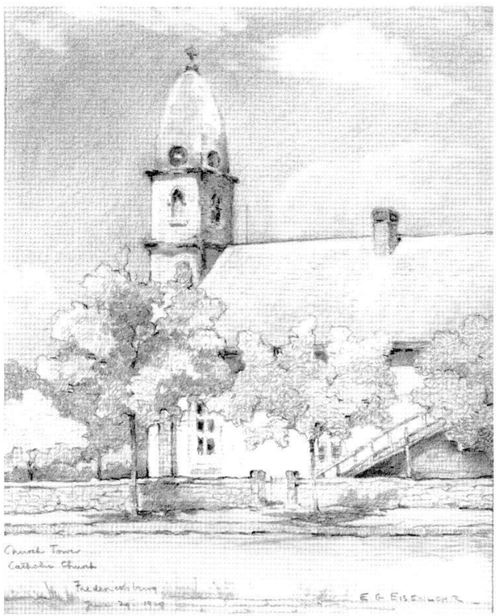

"CHURCH TOWER"
BY EDWARD G. EISENLOHR
10 1/2" x 8" PENCIL DRAWING - JUNE 1928
Courtesy of the Gillespie County Commissioners Court and the McDermott Building Oversight Committee, Fredericksburg, Texas

Because of its eventual settlement and development by more than 30 major ethnic groups from around the world, Texas is a showcase of diverse architectural forms. Fredericksburg's Fort Martin Scott, when restoration is complete, will be an outstanding example of this.

Archaeologists say it was the most "ethnic" fort of the dozens that were built in Texas. The expertise of the German stone-cutters is evident. It also was among the best constructed, thanks to the talents of German masons and carpenters. The Mexican influence is represented in the *jacales*, the thatched-roof huts with upright walls of poles covered with mud and clay.

In different areas of Texas we can still see vestiges of Indian, Spanish, English, French, Swedish and other types of architecture brought here by immigrants. Examples of German architecture are found in many areas of Central Texas. It is in Fredericksburg, however, that the greatest variety of the work of these builders has been preserved. As a living museum of mid-19th Century German architecture, Fredericksburg has no peer in Texas.

This is one of the charms that attracts visitors from all over. Only by looking back at what those before us have accomplished can we come to a new and better understanding of our heritage.

This is particularly true of the "Sunday houses," as much a work of art as a landscape of Hermann Lungkwitz or a sketch by Richard Petri, both of whom brought their considerable talents here early on.

These small structures, which served as little more than hotel accomodations for overnight stays, were relatively late-comers. Most true Sunday houses were built in the 1890's and later by farmers as week-end retreats. The usual routine called for farm families to drive into town on Friday afternoon, spend Saturday buying provisions and then attending church on Sunday before returning home.

The usual Sunday house had a small porch, one large room downstairs and a second on the floor above. They were connected by an exterior stairway. A few had an additional room, particularly if the family was large.

Although the Sunday house is a Fredericksburg trademark, most of the local architecture, as in other Texas German communities, can be traced to the region of that country from which the settlers came. Three different geographic and political areas of Germany furnished the majority of the immigrants. The architecture of each is somewhat distinctive, primarily because of variations in German terrain and climate. Central Germany furnished the bulk of Fredericksburg's settlers and it is that area that had the greatest influence on the design and materials used in the homes they built here.

The settlers put up structures more substantial than the Sunday house as their permanent residence, whether they lived within the town limits or in the hills that surround it. A sizeable number of these places have survived.

An excellent example is the house of John Peter Tatsch. Built in 1852, it still stands after almost a century and a half at the corner of North Bowie and West Schubert. It is representative of the stone houses built by many of the settlers.

Fachwerk (half-timber) houses were common in his homeland, and his choice of stone rather than wood and plaster for his Fredericksburg home likely was dictated by the lack of forests here. Like his neighbors, Tatsch had few tools, and stone may have been easier to fashion than wood. Either material, however, required hard work and expertise in building.

To make the stones fit, he either had to hand pick them for size and surface smoothness, or else chip them to conformity, using whatever tool was available. After more than a century, the rocks used in the house still fit perfectly.

Once the houses were finished, many Texas settlers added a gazebo. These diminutive "garden" houses, open on all sides, are not a German tradition. Rather they are as old as recorded history. They were common in ancient China, but didn't get to Europe until Marco Polo brought the idea back from his travels. After one was erected in Wurzburg in the 1600's, they were an immediate hit in Germany. German immigrants introduced the gazebo to Texas.

Although these roofed structures, usually round or octagon shaped, were never intended as a form of architectural art, many have become so. The addition of intricate lattice-work designs has added a touch of unique artistry to an edifice whose primary purpose was to provide a comfortable place to relax and gaze on the surrounding beauty of nature.

The gazebo remains a fixture today in towns with a German heritage. The Fredericksburg gazebo (which sits in a small park behind the Pioneer Memorial Library) is at least 75 years old. It is used for speeches, band concerts and other activities. During the summer months, concerts by visiting musicians are staged there regularly.

The gazebo is only one example of how man has created art through the use of wood. It has been so throughout recorded history. The Bible tells how King Solomon, in building the temple, "carved all the walls of the house round about with figures of cherubim and palm trees and open flowers within and without." During the Renaissance, Michelangelo and Donatello executed art work from wood for churches and palaces in Italy. It was in Germany, however, that this art form reached new highs and it is to them that we owe a debt of gratitude for bringing wood carving to Texas.

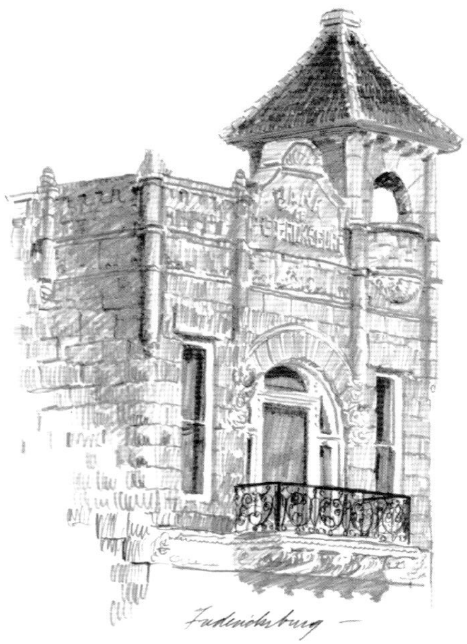

DETAIL FROM PENCIL SKETCH
BY CHARLES BECKENDORF
Courtesy of Charles Beckendorf Gallery

Folk Art

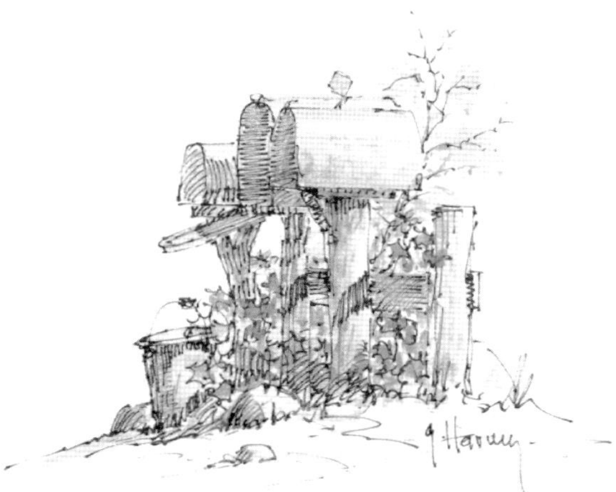

DRAWING BY G. HARVEY ©
Courtesy of G. Harvey

Using wood to create art was not the intention of those trying to establish a new life in Fredericksburg. Most were artisans who saw trees primarily as a source to provide practical household needs such as items of furniture. That some of their work would be lauded a century later as "art" would have surprised the likes of John Peter Tatsch.

Tatsch and his neighbors, long used to turning trees from their forested homeland into beautiful furniture, managed to do the same thing with trees native to this area. Hackberry, black walnut, cherry, cedar and mesquite went into chairs, bedsteads and other furnishings.

Tatsch was a master craftsman at working with wood. In the living room of his home, he built a closet which doubled as a medicine chest and a safe in which to keep important papers. For it he made a highly polished wooden door which, after decades of service, still fits air tight.

For the bedrooms he built two bedsteads---one of hackberry and one of black walnut---that are considered works of art. From cherry he fashioned his masterpiece---a wardrobe that stands six feet high, four feet wide and two feet deep. He decorated each piece with intricate, delicate carvings.

The wives and daughters of these immigrants also were artisans, but in different mediums. Within a year after their arrival, the women of the community had begun to demonstrate their artistic talents. Trained by their German mothers as seamstresses, they converted scraps from dress-making material into crazy quilts of unique design, and dazzling bonnets to protect them from the Texas sun. Needlework was developed into a fine art. Some of their tapestries have survived after a century and a half.

Earliest records do not identify any of Meusebach's first settlers as professional artists. Seth Eastman, the soldier artist, came in 1848. Hermann Lungkwitz and Richard Petri, the first professionals to reside here, did not arrive until 1850. Meusebach's first settlers may not have been trained in art, but paint they did. Many made their homes bright and colorful by decorating walls and ceilings (and sometimes the exteriors) with designs of their own making. As might be expected, some were crude. Others, however, demonstrated considerable talent as to form and the use of color.

Artisans Today

Such "folk" art, if that is a proper name for it, has been passed on to each generation as a part of Fredericksburg life. Many such artisans ply their trade today, their work one of the attractions enjoyed by the town's visitors.

Jeep Collins is famous throughout the country for the unusual jewelry he designs and makes. Fanciers from all over come to see Susan Gaston's wall hangings made from animal skulls and other natural materials. David Karp, who turns out collectible furniture, makes huge chandeliers of copper, cactus and the antlers of deer.

Jonas Perkins is known throughout Texas for his sculpture. Two of his most recent pieces were unveiled in 1995. One is a statue of José Antonio Navarro, a native of Spain and a prominent figure in the Texas Revolution. The other is a bronze statue of Ludwig Boerne, the German reformer who died before he could emigrate to America, but for whom the town of Boerne was named. Perkins has a studio near Fredericksburg.

Bob Marsh is a glass-blower. He turns molten glass into a variety of delicate objects.

Sue Wheeler, a comparative newcomer to Fredericksburg, has turned fine paintings into a kind of folk art that is selling all over the world. Her exquisite 5x7-inch paintings (done in gouache, an opaque water color), include animals, old buildings, gardens and nostalgic scenes. Some have become plates distributed by the Bradford Exchange, including a Christmas series for collectors. She has been asked to design one of four plates commemorating the 150th anniversary of Fredericksburg in 1996.

Her work adorns greeting cards distributed by one of the nation's largest companies. She also has produced an entire line of "baby" art that includes birth announcements, a calendar, a growth chart, mugs and more. Now Sue Wheeler original paintings are also attracting buyers.

Rex White and Fred Muegge fashion lovely, functional furniture in the traditional design. Finn Alban's pottery is featured in shows around the state.

In June, 1995, White, Muegge and Alban, among others, induced some of Fredericksburg's and the Hill Country's best artists and artisans to participate in an event they now plan to be an annual affair. They staged the Fredericksburg Artists Invitational Show and Sale. The show featured pottery, furniture, paintings, engravings, jewelry, iron work, textiles, photography, silversmiths, woodworking and folk art.

These are but representative examples of dozens of artists and craftsmen in this city where art in many forms has been a part of daily life for a century and a half.

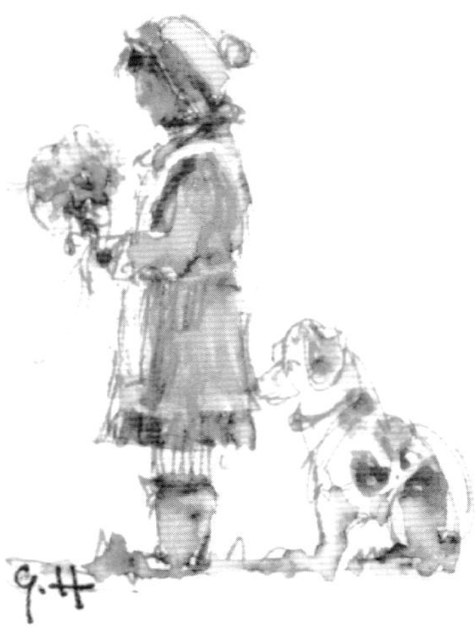

DRAWING BY G. HARVEY ©
Courtesy of G. Harvey

It's May Day Every Day

Some variety of folk art is apparent everywhere in Fredericksburg. One of the most unusual pieces (and the one seen by thousands of visitors) is the *Maibaum* (Maypole) on *Marktplatz*, the central town square.

May Day---May 1---is a traditional celebration in Germany, particularly Bavaria. Decades ago the villagers there erected May Poles for Spring festivals and later used them to display symbols of the local history, commerce or other matters of interest concerning the village. The May Pole became a kind of local archive.

In 1991, when the Pedernales Creative Arts Alliance was looking for a meaningful contribution to the redevelopment of the town square, it hit on a unique idea. Members asked Roy Bellows, a local artisan who is an expert with iron, to create a May Pole with figures that would relate the history of Fredericksburg.

For the pole, Bellows used the trunk of the burr oak---a species that is notable for its stately height and durability. The trunk and branches are wrought iron and the leaves are copper with a natural patina. Each of the branches uses figures to depict a bit of the town's history.

The bottom branch portrays the peace negotiations conducted with the Comanche Indians by John O. Meusebach, Fredericksburg's founder, on March 2, 1847. The agreement allowed the new colony to develop in peace.

With peace assured, figures of ranchers and dancing couples are depicted celebrating on the second level. The third level, or branch, represents the grapes and peaches, vital to the town's economy; the next shows hunters stalking deer, turkey and the abundant wild game.

Sheep, goats and cattle, mainstays of Fredericksburg's agriculture for a century and a half, graze on the next branch. The ship and ox cart on the next portray the arrival of the original settlers who landed at Indianola, then carted their possessions overland to their new home.

The "Sunday houses" they built and the Nimitz Hotel (today the Admiral Nimitz Museum) decorate the next level. The devotion of the settlers to the Christian faith are symbolized by tiny replicas of the Vereins Kirche and Cross Mountain on the highest level. Topping the *Maibaum* are 12 branches of the burr oak.

Although Bellows' work is a highlight of the renovated *Marktplatz*, art in iron is no stranger to other Fredericksburg welders. Kermit Boos & Sons, Rode's Iron and Pipe Yard, James Klinksiek Welding Co. and others produce work of artistic quality. Many of the ornate gates that welcome visitors to Hill Country ranches were designed and built by them.

Although ranch owners themselves lay no claim to being artists or professional ironmongers, some are expert in this genre. On cold winter days they break the monotony of feeding livestock by turning to their forge and making their own gates.

The Limners

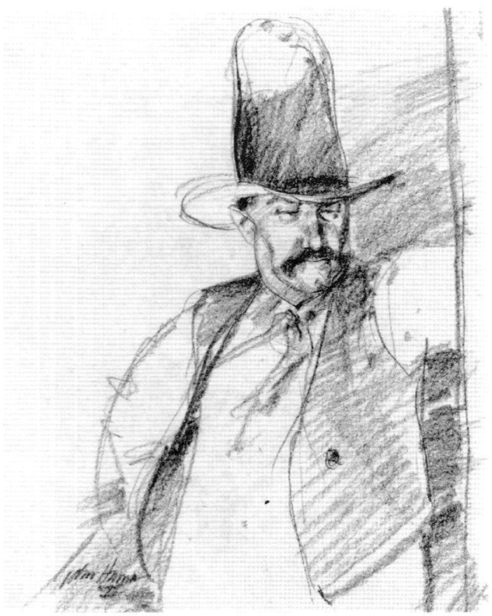

PENCIL SKETCH BY JOHN AUSTIN HANNA
Courtesy of John and Sherrie Hanna

Whether it was the work of the artisans or the fable that the new settlers in Fredericksburg had money to spend on "art" isn't known, but soon the town was invaded by a succession of painters who called themselves "illuminers" or limners."

"Illuminers" were respectable artisans in the mid-19th Century. The term originally described anyone who painted armorial bearings, carriages, coaches, houses and even signs. Later many expanded their talent and became "face painters." In some ways, the "limner" was akin to the modern artists who people areas like the River Walk in San Antonio and draw or paint caricatures of those willing to spend a half hour's time and a few dollars.

The limners who plied their trade between the Comal and the Pedernales Rivers had a different clientele. They traveled by horseback or buggy, visiting farms and going door-to-door in villages like Fredericksburg soliciting families to sit for "portraits." In a time when the camera was still a crude device and photographers were a rarity, limners were the portraitists for the common man.

Virtually every settler wanted a family portrait. They welcomed the limner because they were affordable and made sitting for a picture as painless as possible.

The limner arrived ready to work. Usually he had prepared in advance a number of canvasses consisting of headless (but dressed) bodies of men, women and children. If the artist knew something in advance of the household, he might arrive with a "family" canvas---one with a headless man, woman and the appropriate children.

Since he had bodies of almost every size and a variety of family groups already finished, painting in the faces was all that was required to complete the "portrait." Sometimes to clinch a sale he would add lace or a pin to a lady's frock or a gold watch chain for the gentleman.

For more affluent clients willing to sit longer and pay more, the limner was delighted to begin with a fresh canvas and do a "face picture" from scratch. In every case, the results became family treasures, displayed in front parlors with pride.

By the start of World War I, the limner had disappeared from the area. He was replaced by photography, chromolithographs, and masses of Currier & Ives prints that provided attractive, but cheap, decorations for homes.

No portraits by limners are included here because their works are unsigned and undated. Several pictures that appear to be painted by limners do appear in the book, *Pioneers in God's Country*, published by the Gillespie County Historical Society in 1974. The limners are important because of their unique contributions to early art here and elsewhere in Texas.

The Coming of the Professionals

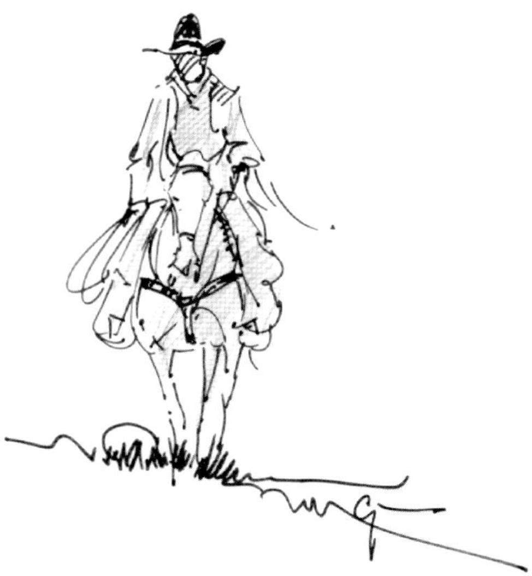

PENCIL SKETCH © BY G. HARVEY
Courtesy of G. Harvey

The first professional artist arrived in Fredericksburg two years after the community was settled. He was Seth Eastman, an artist from Maine, whose specialty was drawing buildings and landscapes for the Army. He came as a soldier rather than an artist.

The *Adelsverein* had located its new town on the Pedernales in Comanche territory and Washington was concerned about protecting settlers in Indian country. Eventually three lines of forts would be built in Texas. The first in the chain was located here on December 5, 1848 and Captain Seth Eastman was assigned to command it. During his few months of service at the fort, the soldier-artist produced a priceless record of some 15 drawings of area scenes.

Other artists soon followed. And while Fredericksburg has never aspired to be another Taos or Santa Fe, its population has always included several prominent painters in residence. Why they selected this German village in the "Hills of God" as a place to live, or just to visit and paint, is easy to understand.

The Hill Country is not typical Texas. It is a harsh land of cedar-clad hills, mesquite brush, rocky terrain and creeks that are mostly dry. It has been called a harsh land because, as historian Walter Prescott Webb said, it has been "burned by drought, beaten by hail, withered by hot winds and frozen by blizzards." Yet, it also is a gentle land of little hills and verdant valleys, of limestone springs and forests of perennially green live oaks mixed with the cedar.

John Graves, one of Texas' favorite writers, has said that "The Hill Country has a charm and a beauty of a sort that somehow tugs at the feelings of people from other, different kinds of country."

It was that appeal that made the German settlers want to make it their home. They realized that the valleys that divided the gentle hills would be productive of good crops, and they were right.

Artists say the area around Fredericksburg gives them a sense of the vast space of Texas. The sky is enormous---as beautiful as the fabled skies of Italy. And they're always an intense blue, except for a few short weeks in winter. To those familiar with the Hill Country, it's the place, deep in the heart of Texas, where the stars shine brightest.

Artists say it is also a place that takes one back in time. Painters say that the light here is transparent. And while El Paso claims to be the sunniest spot in the state, the sun seems to shine brighter and longer in "God's hills" than anywhere else.

A century and a half after Seth Eastman was enchanted and mystified by these valleys, streams and hills, many other artists have followed him to Fredericksburg. Although its physical beauty has been a major attraction in drawing them here, so have the German traditions that have made it a mecca for tourists.

The Sound of Music

From its beginnings, the residents have shown an interest in nurturing all of the arts---especially music. It has been said that the Germans have taught the world to sing. As one writer puts it: "They have carried music into the homes, the school rooms, the treeless wilds, the remote forests and before the greatest audiences in the world."

The settlers who had no other artistic talents seemed to be blessed with beautiful voices, and singing was integral to daily living. The first *Saengerbund* (singing society) was organized March 2, 1850, at New Braunfels. Soon there were others in Fredericksburg, Sisterdale and the other German communities. The first *Saengerfest* (convention of *Saengerbunds*) was held in New Braunfels. The sixth was hosted by Fredericksburg.

Musical talents extended beyond singing. On October 15, 1858, Frank Valentin van der Stucken was born in Fredericksburg. His parents, a Belgian father and a German mother, both loved music. When young Frank showed signs of musical genius early on, the family moved to Belgium so he could be exposed to the best teachers in Europe.

By the age of 16, van der Stucken had composed two original works. He went on to compose many symphonies and the music for a production of Shakespeare's *The Tempest*. In 1889, at the World Exposition in Paris, he conducted the first European concert in history to feature an entire program of American music.

In 1895, when Mrs. William Howard Taft and others founded the Cincinnati Symphony, Van der Stucken was named its musical director, and became its conductor the next year, a post he held until 1907.

Van der Stucken never returned to his birthplace, but his memory is still honored here each year with a special concert sponsored by the van der Stucken Foundation.

Fredericksburg's current composer-in-residence is 35-year-old Mark Hierholzer, music director at Zion Lutheran Church and accompanist for the Fredericksburg Chorale, the Children's Chorale and other musical groups.

He also teaches piano, but his first love is composing. A New York publisher has brought out some of the traditional cowboy tunes that he arranged for the Children's Chorale. When that group presented its 10th anniversary concert in 1995, a highlight was Hierholzer's "Mass in E Minor." As his works are being performed by more musical groups in other cities around the nation, he intends to find more time to compose.

One reason Hierholzer, his wife and their four children prefer to live in Fredericksburg is because of the rich musical talent here. The two chorales---the adult and the children's---are prime examples. Both were organized in 1985 by Laurie Jenschke, a native of Fredericksburg. Her groups have won acclaim throughout the state.

Membership in the choirs reflects the love of music that remains a heritage in the community. The dentist and the retired banker, the math teacher and the mother of four, the insurance agent and the artist---the 50 singers represent a cross section of interests and ages.

The Children's Chorale began with 22 students; now there are 110.

Singing is a tradition in Fredericksburg. For those who aren't members of the Chorale, there is the Sons of Herman Choir, a prestigious group that has played an important role in the town's musical culture for many years. When the community gathers for events like *Oktoberfest* and *Kriskindl*, singing always has a role. *Saengerfests* are still as important today as they were a century and a half ago.

Duncan Holmes, Fredericksburg's talented and personable blind pianist, entertains at local churches, nursing homes, schools, restaurants and other group gatherings, and also travels around the country to perform.

On the lighter side, there are the German "oom-pah" bands to play for dancing and festivals, and country western groups for those who prefer the Texas two-step.

For those who want to make their own music at home, Fredericksburg provides a unique way. John and Shirley Naylor manufacture dulcimers in one of the largest factories of its kind in the United States. They assemble the melodious stringed instruments in a variety of shapes and colors and even provide introductory lessons for aspiring dulcimer players.

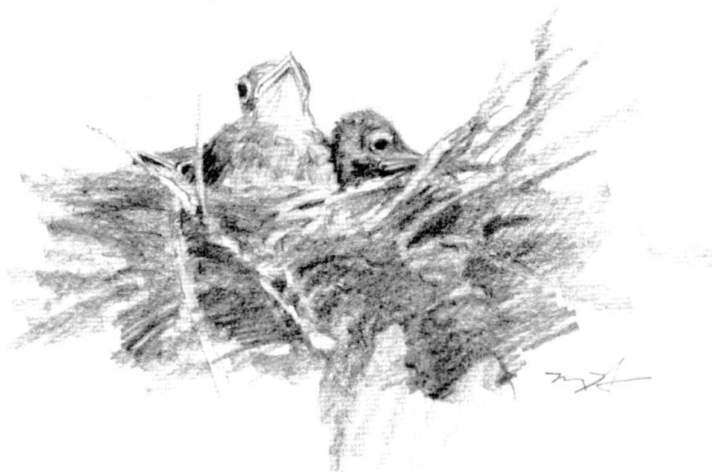

"CARDINALS"
PENCIL SKETCH BY MARK HAWORTH
Courtesy of Mark Haworth

Where the Arts are at Home

Of the many traditions the German settlers brought with them to Texas, the appreciation of fine arts was among the most important and lasting. The affection for, and support of, the arts continues to be a part of everyday life in Fredericksburg.

The first formally organized group was the Casino Society, started in 1886 "for the cultivation of the fine arts, especially the dramatic and musical arts, and the intellectual stimulation of its members." It was affiliated with a similar organization in San Antonio.

The Fredericksburg Art Guild, now more than a quarter of a century old, was formed on a dare!

In 1970, John McClusky, a well-known Connecticut artist, moved to Fredericksburg. Soon he paid a courtesy call at Ko-Art & Music, a local gallery operated by Irene Kowert. She asked him for lessons. He refused, politely pointing out that she couldn't afford his fees.

"But," he said, "if you will find 20 people who want to learn to paint in acrylic, I will give you all lessons for free."

Irene easily found 20 prospective students. She then induced the town fathers to donate space in a warehouse for a classroom and the Fredericksburg Art Guild was born. Classes met each Monday night with McClusky teaching. When the city reclaimed the warehouse space three years later, the Guild rented space above Dooley's Five, Ten and Twenty-Five Cent Store on Main Street and classes continued.

John McClusky believed that everybody owed a debt to the place where they live. His free lessons were his way of paying his obligation to his adopted home town. Over the years, he taught more than 200 students---many of them busy mothers of small children--the rudiments of art.

In 1980, the group organized officially. On January 26, 1981 the Fredericksburg Art Guild was approved as a non-profit organization and McClusky, Irene Kowert and Dorothy Stehling were elected as directors.

McClusky's philosophy of giving something back to the community remains the credo of the Guild. Dorothy Stehling, Tamara Korman and Ruby Lee Clark painted the replica of the Nimitz Hotel used as scenery in the Annual Easter Fires Pageant. Dorothy Stehling has painted backdrops for the Gillespie County Fair parade floats. As a project of *Die Künstler*, Willie Mae Moerbe, Iris Britton, Jo Ann Tanner, Zella Morgan, Dorothy Mansen, Dorothy Stehling, Tamara Korman and Janice Langerhans painted scenery for an intermediate school musical.

Nancy Coon, an artist whose works include a variety of styles and types of painting, has done sketches for the Pioneer Memorial Library. With the help of other artist friends, she painted the mural that decorates the town's Municipal Swimming Pool.

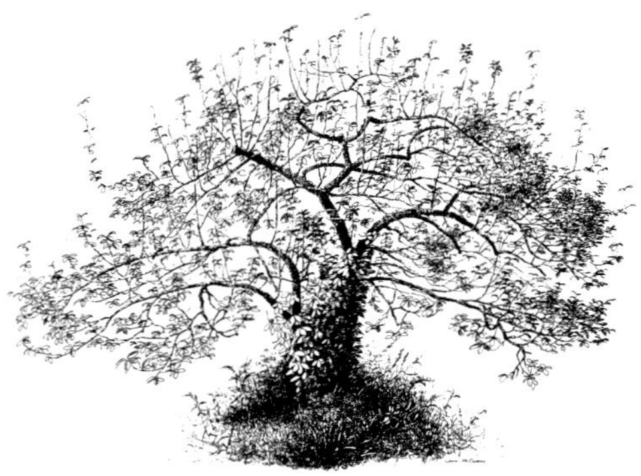

"APPLE TREE"
BY JOHN McCLUSKY
PEN AND INK DRAWING
Courtesy of Mrs. John McClusky

McClusky died in 1994, but the Fredericksburg Art Guild continues to meet weekly and still teaches acrylic painting.

Meanwhile local recognition of the importance of the arts to the community continues to grow. In 1979, two years before the Fredericksburg Art Guild was formally incorporated, the Pedernales Creative Arts Alliance was organized. No local group has done more to promote all of the arts. Members are not content to limit their concerns to the so-called "fine arts" like painting and music. Their purpose is to encourage and support 55 different forms of art in 11 separate categories!

There was a good reason for such an ambitious approach. Professional artists were in residence, but so were a host of Sunday painters, weavers, writers, potters, puppeteers and a variety of others. The goal of PCAA is to provide a productive environment for any and all endeavors related to the arts.

In November, 1979, the PCAA opened its own gallery. Sarah Harle and Lee Ethel, both resident painters, were named co-directors. The purpose of the gallery was to provide an outlet where all artists could make their works visible to the public. At one point, the organization seriously considered purchasing a Main Street building as a permanent home for its headquarters and gallery.

Those plans did not materialize, but the PCAA continued to grow in membership, importance, and in the scope of its activities. In 1981, it sponsored Oktoberfest, a celebration reminiscent of the world famous one in Munich. Professional artists, artisans of every description, musical groups, craftsmen, hobbyists---any and all who had even a tenuous tie with art were invited to participate.

The result was a unique event that has continued to grow in stature, quality and support each year. Thousands crowd Fredericksburg on the weekend of *Oktoberfest* to see the best in area art, to listen and sing to oom-pah band music and to dance the polkas that the Meusebach colony introduced so long ago.

In the Fall of 1992, a group of local artists felt that there was a need for another organization that would unite the visual arts in Fredericksburg. They met with Peter Fox, president of the Texas Arts Council, and the *Die Künstler von Fredericksburg* was the result.

The German name was chosen because of the town's heritage and to honor the memory of Hermann Lungkwitz and Richard Petri who, in 1850, became the first formally educated artists from that country to make Fredericksburg their home.

Die Künstler's goals: "To promote the highest aesthetic standards in visual art; to promote art education in the public schools, colleges and the general public; to preserve the German heritage through the visual arts; to create and sponsor workshops beneficial to area artists; to encourage the development of artistic talents; to offer a forum for exhibition and sale for local artists, and to create a visual arts

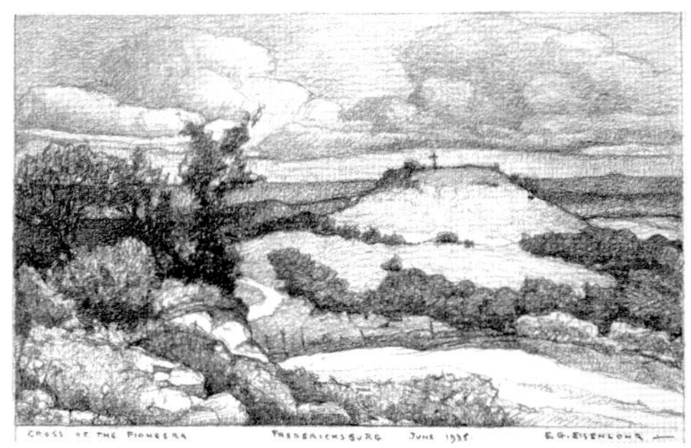

DETAIL FROM PENCIL DRAWING OF
"THE CROSS OF THE PIONEERS"
BY EDWARD G. EISENLOHR
10" x 14" PENCIL
Courtesy of the Gillespie County Commissioners Court and the McDermott Building Oversight Committee, Fredericksburg, Texas

library."

It is this kind of community support that has attracted artists to Fredericksburg over the years, not only to live here, but to visit. In his introduction to Mondell Rogers' book, *Old Ranches of the Texas Plains*, Mitchell A. Wilder wrote:

"A visit to Fredericksburg might be likened to foreign travel. It carries you back in place and time."

Porfirio Salinas, the late San Antonio artist famous for his paintings of bluebonnets, never lived here, but this area of the Hill Country was one of his favorite subjects. The artist said this about the Hill Country:

"There's a magic about it that holds people to it no matter how high up they go. It's like returning to your father's house. You feel safe, protected, loved---as if you were really important."

A part of that magic is *Marktplatz*, the central square laid out by Meusebach and now a work of visual art itself. In recent years, the city has spent some $3 million to build covered pavilions and a history walk and to restore the grounds to a "green area." It has always been the heart of Fredericksburg. A replica of the *Vereins Kirche*, which served as both church and school for the settlers, still stands. In 1896, on the town's 50th birthday, the square truly became *Festplatz*, the festival place, and has remained so.

The setting has always impressed visitors. In 1847, Dr. F. Roemer, the famed German geologist, wrote after visiting the year-old village:

"Coming to Fredericksburg, when following Main Street, one sees Market Square which appears to be large enough to accommodate a city of ten to twelve thousand inhabitants..."

Roemer would be astonished today to know that more thousands than that gather on *Marktplatz* for events like *Oktoberfest*. He would be even more surprised to find that it is the town's annual showcase of its art that attracts these crowds.

For a century and a half, Fredericksburg has nurtured artists. Cecelia Steinfeldt, senior curator of the San Antonio Museum Association, says that there were three significant painters among the German immigrants in the 1840's. They were G. von Iwonski, Hermann Lungkwitz and Richard Petri.

Two of them---Lungkwitz and Petri---made Fredericksburg their home.

In the decades since, all types of artists have continued to choose Fredericksburg. The stories of some of them, from 1846 through 1995, are chronicled in the pages that follow.

Biographies

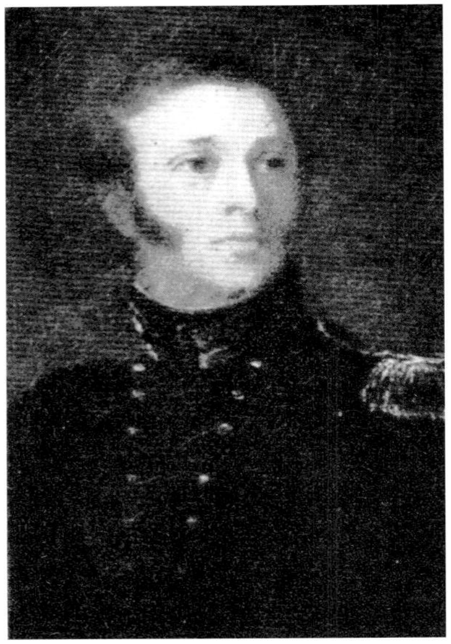

SETH EASTMAN
1808-1875
"The Soldier Artist"

Seth Eastman came to Fredericksburg two years after its founding and made at least 15 sketches of the town and its surroundings. They are the earliest pictorial records of the settlement, and among the most valuable in existence.

Happenstance had brought him to Texas. A West Point graduate (1829) and a career Army officer, his assignment was to investigate and make sketches of Indian life on the frontier. At the military academy, he had studied topographical drawing and landscape painting.

When the Bureau of Indian Affairs was ordered to "collect and prepare for publication the history, condition and prospects of the Indian tribes in the U.S.," Eastman sought the appointment as illustrator. He didn't get it. Instead 2nd Lt. Eastman served briefly at a couple of forts, was promoted to captain and fought in the Florida War. Then he was brought back to West Point to teach art.

Nearing the age of 40, he already had made a minor reputation as a painter with his sketches and water colors of Hudson River landscapes. Despite his avowed interest in Indians, only occasionally did he include them in these early works. Nevertheless he welcomed an assignment to Fort Snelling, Minnesota, where he made hundreds of sketches of Indian life.

In October, 1848, Eastman and his Co. D of the First Infantry Regiment were ordered to New Orleans, with the Rio Grande their eventual destination. Orders were changed, however, and Eastman and his men were dispatched to take command of Fort Martin Scott near Fredericksburg.

Earlier the Army had located Camp Houston east of the two-year-old German settlement established by Baron von Meusebach in the Pedernales River Valley. With the ever increasing threat of Indian attacks, however, the Army decided to upgrade the post to a fort---the first in a tier that would be built to protect the West. It was renamed for Lt. Col. Martin Scott who had been killed in the war with Mexico.

On the march north from Indianola to Fredericksburg, Eastman and his troops paused in San Antonio. He was not favorably impressed with the town, but remained long enough to sketch the Missions and a view of the Main Plaza from the watch tower. Later he turned these sketches into renderings in water colors and oil.

Although San Antonio left him unimpressed, he was enthralled by Fredericksburg, calling it "a very fine country full of game and Indians." However, getting to what he described as "the Dutch settlement" wasn't easy. He wrote in his journal:

"(We) left San Antonio with 47 soldiers (seven sick), eight wagons, nine teamsters, one wagon master, 20 days' provisions and ten days of courage." Both their provisions and their courage lasted, however, and they arrived at Fort Martin Scott on December 2.

Eastman was ecstatic with his new post and especially pleased with the

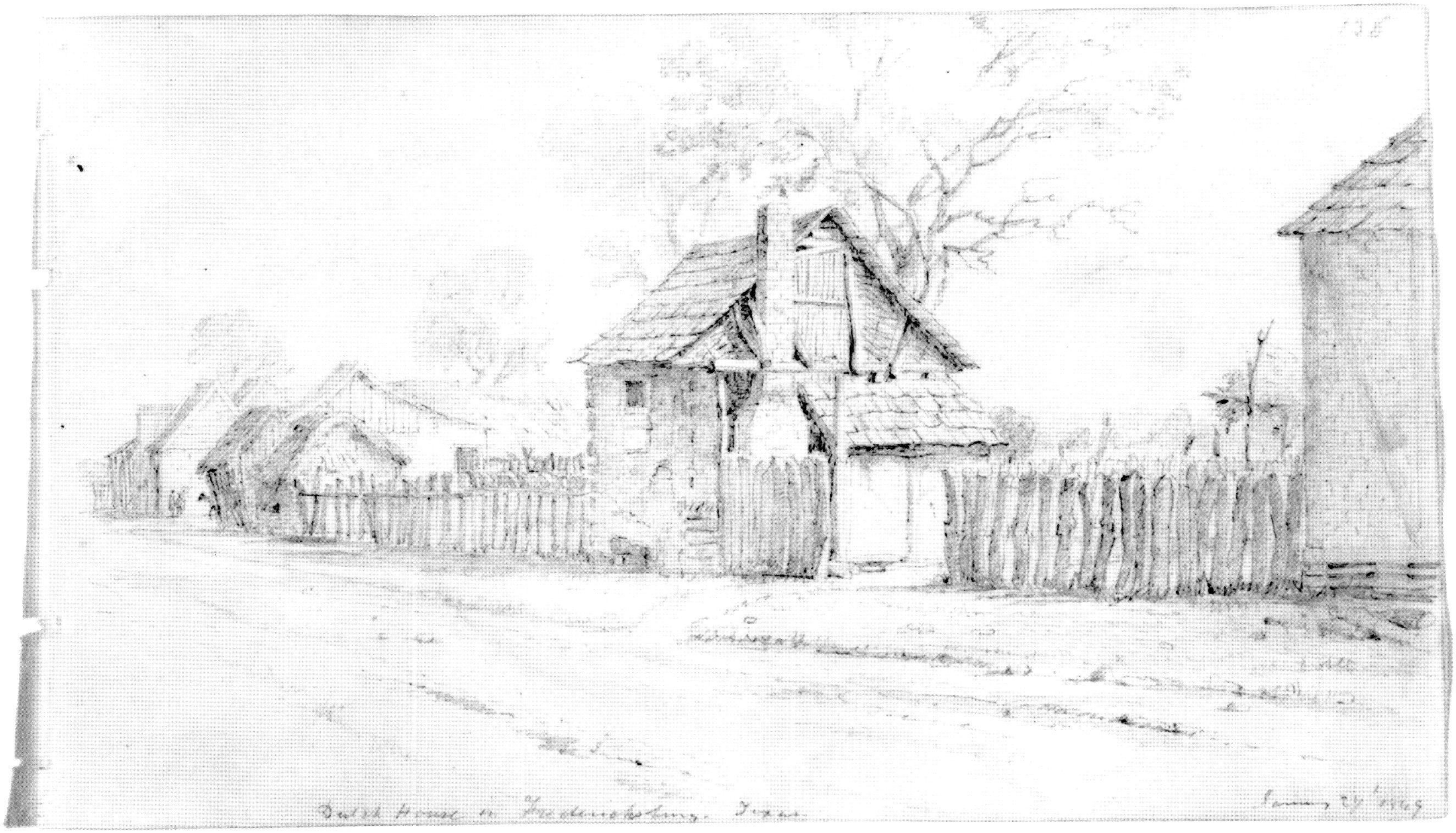

"DUTCH HOUSE IN FREDERICKSBURG, TEXAS
JANUARY 27, 1849"
BY SETH EASTMAN
GRAPHITE ON PAPER
From the Collection of
the McNay Art Museum, San Antonio, Texas
Gift of the Pearl Brewing Company

proximity of Indians. A week after his arrival, he wrote his friend, Col. Henry S. Sibley, delegate to Congress from Minnesota:

"Besides the Cumanches (Comanches), we have the Delawares, Shawnees, Wakoos (probably Wacos) and Lassan (Lipan) Indians." He added that he already had set up a meeting with Santa Anna, the Comanche chief. He failed to point out, however, that getting the shy tribesmen to pose for his sketches was not easy.

Since Indian models were in short supply, Eastman emphasized landscapes and buildings. Intrigued by what he called "the Dutch houses," he sketched many of them in pencil. Scenes of Fort Martin Scott and the surrounding area provided him with many subjects. He did a delicate pencil drawing of the *Vereins Kirche*, the old church. He painted a hunting scene near Fredericksburg in oil.

The collection of Eastman's work owned by the Witte Museum in San Antonio includes a 4x7-inch watercolor titled "View in Texas about 65 miles North of San Antonio". Apparently it was made near Camp Houston (now Fort Martin Scott) and is a broad vista of Texas landscape with few colors in the diminutive space. It is believed that he used it as a kind of "post card" to his wife to illustrate the vastness of the land in which he was serving.

Modern artists marvel at the volume of his work done under conditions hardly inspiring to good art. Sketches predominate, probably because he had to do most of them while sitting on a horse. Also it was difficult for a mounted soldier on active duty to carry many painting tools. Only later, when surroundings were more favorable, was he able to put some of his sketches into oils and water colors.

The Sketch Book, in which he also detailed his experiences in prose, contained 70 Texas drawings, including the 15 of Fredericksburg and the hills around it. Nine were of San Antonio subjects, two of Seguin and five of Matagorda Bay and Indianola. The others were scenes of landscapes throughout the area. Once again, however, Indians were almost non-existent in his work.

Eastman did not seem discouraged by the fact that while there were hundreds of Indians around Fredericksburg and Fort Martin Scott, he was not getting drawings of them into his sketch book. No matter. His opportunity would come.

In 1850, his dream of using his expertise on Indians came true. On February 27, 1850, he was ordered to Washington by the War Department to assist the Office of Indian Affairs in completing the work it had started before his Texas tour of duty. His assignment was to illustrate the six volumes of Henry Rowe Schoolcraft's *Historical and Standard Information Respecting the History, Conditions and Prospects of Indian Tribes in the United States*. The job took him four years to complete. As might be expected, none of his Texas sketches were included.

Eastman hadn't given up on sketching Texas Indians, however. When his illustrations for Schoolcraft's volumes were completed in 1854, Eastman returned to

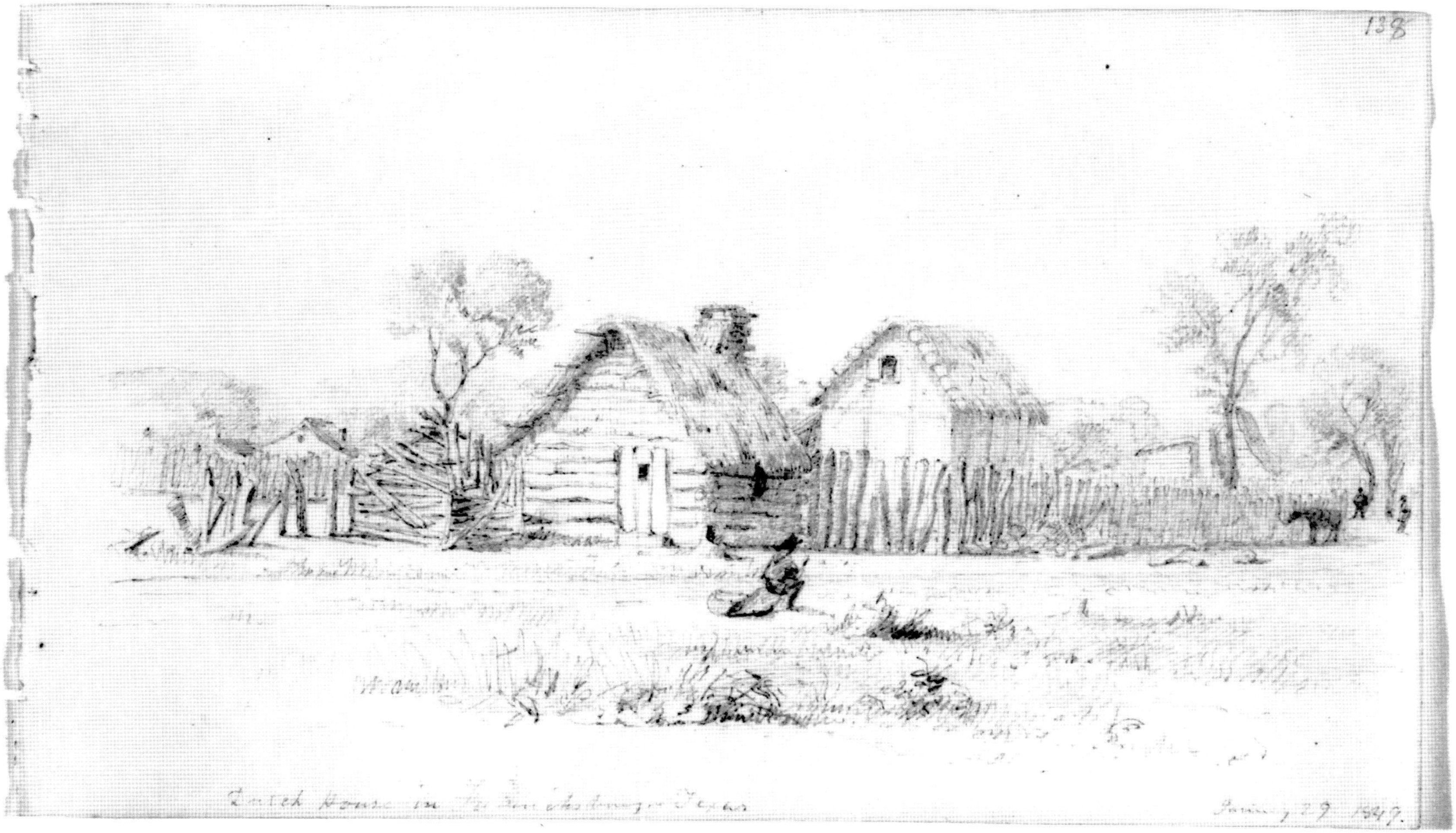

"DUTCH HOUSE IN FREDERICKSBURG, TEXAS
JANUARY 29, 1849"
BY SETH EASTMAN
GRAPHITE ON PAPER
From the Collection of
the McNay Art Museum, San Antonio, Texas
Gift of the Pearl Brewing Company

Texas the next year.

He was stationed first at Fort Duncan, above Eagle Pass on the Rio Grande, and later at Fort Chadbourne in Coke County. Fort Martin Scott was still an active military post (it remained so until December 28, 1866), but there is no record that he made a return visit to the fort or the town whose early history he had done so much to preserve in his sketches and his prose.

Eastman retired from active duty in 1863 but continued on modified service. In 1867, the Army breveted him a major general. His assignment was to paint oils of native American scenes and U.S. forts. Still working on the project when he died in 1875, he had completed 26 of the paintings. They hang today in the Capitol in Washington.

He is buried in Washington, D.C.

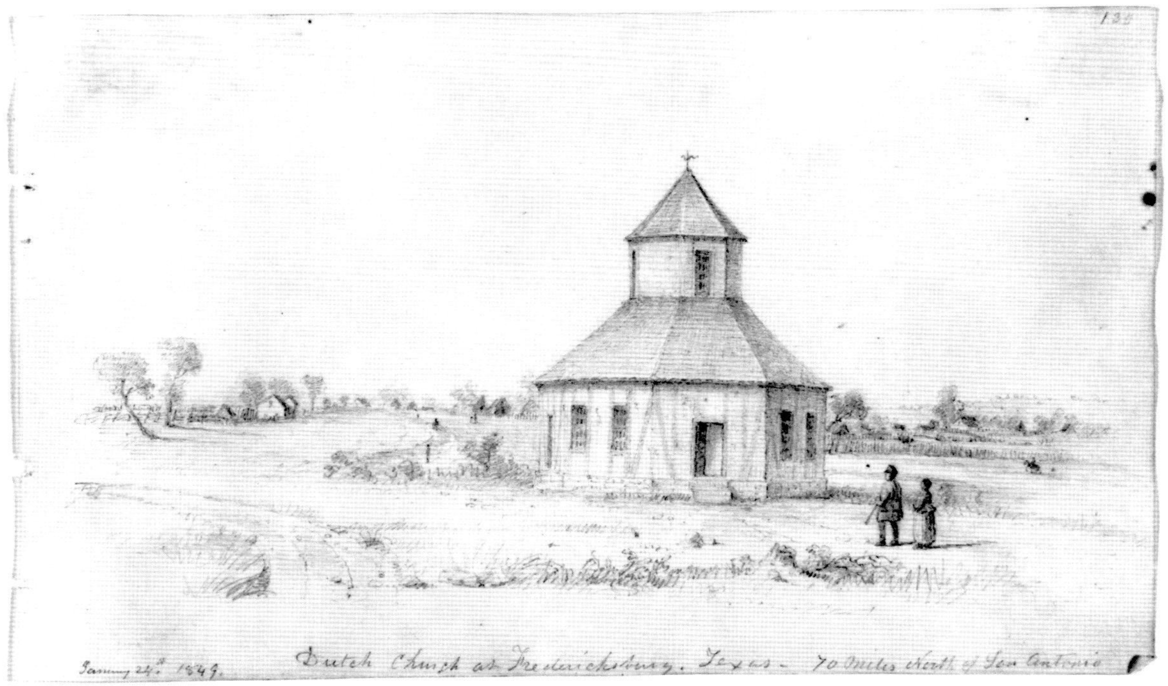

"DUTCH CHURCH AT FREDERICKSBURG, TEXAS -
70 MILES NORTH OF SAN ANTONIO, JANUARY 24, 1849"
BY SETH EASTMAN
Collection of the McNay Art Museum, San Antonio, Texas
Gift of the Pearl Brewing Company

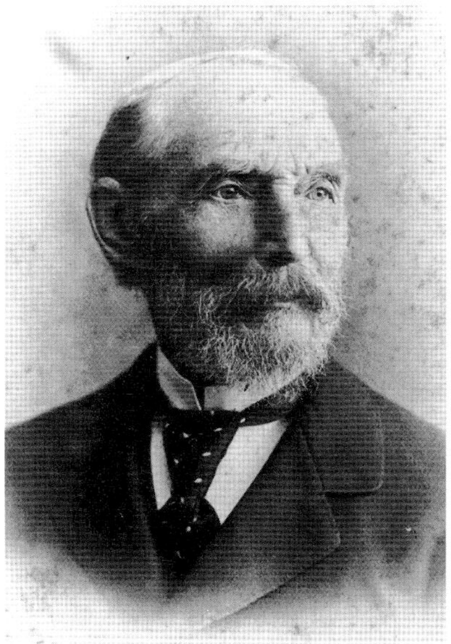

HERMANN LUNGKWITZ
1813-1891
"The Farmer Artist"

Photo Courtesy of Institute of Texan Cultures, The University of Texas at San Antonio

He was the only academic-trained artist in Texas for almost a generation, yet he died virtually unknown outside of Fredericksburg, Austin and San Antonio.

He was Hermann Lungkwitz, farmer, photographer and part-time artist who managed to leave more than 300 exquisite drawings and paintings when he died in 1891. More than half of these were produced during his 40-year residence in Fredericksburg and Central Texas.

March 14, 1813 is a day still remembered in his native Halle an der Salle, Germany, but not because it is Lungkwitz's birth date. The Napoleonic Wars were in full swing, and fighting was going on all around Halle on the day he was born to the wife of a successful manufacturer of hosiery.

Except for economic pressures, the war had little effect on the life of the Lungkwitz family. The business prospered and Johann Gottfried Lungkwitz hoped that Hermann, the second of five children, would follow him in the hosiery business someday. However, young Hermann showed early talent as an artist---a trait that displeased the elder Lungkwitz. Thus no effort was made to train the youngster in art.

Indeed, Hermann might have been forced into a career of turning prime wool into hosiery except for a happenstance. A rich uncle died leaving a legacy that allowed him to enroll in the *Akademie de Bildenden Kunste* (Royal Academy) at Dresden. He was 25, already a self-taught artist. He also was a political rebel who had fought against an autocratic King.

Although his start at the Academy was late, it was a pleasant episode in a life that often was filled with disappointment and heartache. In Germany, he managed to sell only a few paintings. His dream was to bring his talent to America where he was confident he could make a contribution to art as well as a good living.

At the Academy, he met Richard Petri, a 14-year-old genius at the easel, and they became fast friends. Later he would marry Petri's sister, Elisabet---"Elise" to her friends. And in 1850, he would bring his wife; his 78-year-old mother; his sister, Therese; and Richard Petri and his sister, Marie, to America and eventually to Texas. His brother, Adolph, a silversmith, would follow soon.

It was not an easy decision. Lungkwitz's father had died and the family fortune had ebbed. His own painting had brought in little money. To pay for their passage to America, his mother sold their household furnishings. It was a pattern of near poverty that would follow him all of his life.

Arriving in America, the two families first stopped in Wheeling, Virginia (now West Virginia). However, the climate was not suitable for his wife or for her brother, Richard, who had tuberculosis. In 1851, they started for Texas---a trip that took four months of travel by train, ship and ox cart before they finally reached New Braunfels.

At that time, New Braunfels had 1,723 residents and was the fourth largest settlement in Texas. They remained there for six months and Hermann managed to sell a couple of paintings and earned $6 for teaching a seminar. However, for reasons never made clear, they decided to move west to the smaller settlement of Fredericksburg.

The two families bought a 320-acre farm for $400. It was on Live Oak Creek near the Pedernales River and close to the grist and saw mill operated by Carl Hilmar Guenther.

Lungkwitz grew a beard and tried to learn something of farming since he had a wife and four children to support. He did, however, manage to paint as well. In 1852, he painted what is believed to be his first Texas landscape---an oil painting of the mill run by his neighbor, Guenther. This was the beginning of his production of many such paintings and drawings of Fredericksburg and the Hill Country---work that has earned him recognition as the "father" of landscape painting in Texas.

Supporting a family through his art, however, proved to be a tough assignment for the pipe-smoking, easy-going painter. He necessarily had to devote much of his time to his crops. Petri, his friend and confidant, was too frail to be of much help at hard, physical labor. Also, he was too busy doing his own sketches and paintings. When Petri drowned in the Pedernales River in 1857, it was an emotional blow to Lungkwitz from which he never recovered.

However, his problems---both personal and economic---did not make him a recluse. He often joined his neighbors for an evening of drinking good beer and conversation. He had a good tenor voice and sang with a Fredericksburg quartet. He enjoyed the theater and acted in some plays after the Nimitz Hotel erected a small stage. He also painted the scenery.

He obviously enjoyed his life in Fredericksburg, but his paintings and sketches didn't sell. Like him, the other burghers had little ready cash. Things worsened with the outbreak of the Civil War. By the war's end, money was so short that Lungkwitz feared he might even lose his farm. He sold off parts of it, keeping only 130 acres. That helped the family fortunes, but not much.

In 1866, he went to San Antonio hoping for better things. There Carl G. Von Iwonski, a Hungarian immigrant and artist, had opened a studio to make portraits with a camera instead of a brush. Iwonski already was a well-established painter, but he saw a new future in photography.

Lungkwitz was enthralled by the new technique. With Iwonski, they produced a magic lantern show that astonished Texans with its "brilliant Stereomonoscopic Dissolving Views and Polaroscopic Fire Works." Their venture was brief, but it was a success.

It also taught Lungkwitz about the use of light and brighter hues in his paintings, which improved his work. His landscapes were no longer drab, but had

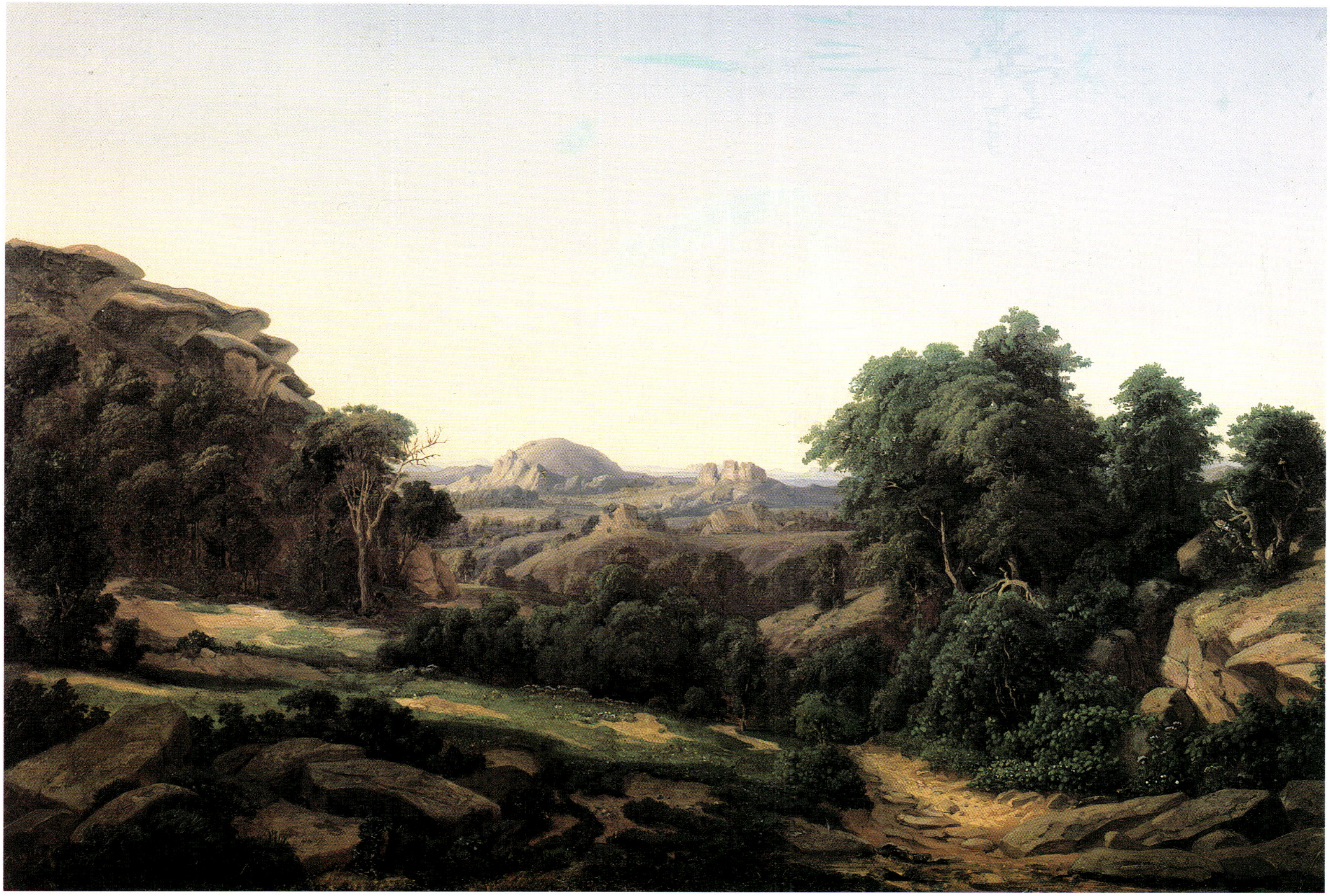

"ENCHANTED ROCK NEAR FREDERICKSBURG"
BY HERMANN LUNGKWITZ 1864
14" X 20" OIL ON CANVAS
Collection of The Witte Museum, San Antonio, Texas

greater finish and brilliance, and they sold well.

Although there was now more demand for his work, Lungkwitz could not depend entirely on his art to support his family. Fortunately he had a close friend who could help. Earlier, Marie Petri had married Jacob Kuechler, a German immigrant who was a surveyor in Fredericksburg. This brought Kuechler into the extended Lungkwitz family and the couple lived on the Lungkwitz farm until 1870.

That year, Kuechler was named Commissioner of the General Land Office of the state of Texas and moved to Austin. He asked Lungkwitz to become the Office's official photographer and produce maps. Lungkwitz also was asked to teach painting in both the English and German schools in the capital.

In 1881, Lungkwitz's beloved Elise died. And when a change in administrations cost him his job as photographer, he took up painting again with renewed interest. The last years of his life, most of which were spent in Austin or on ranches where he lived with friends, were his most productive. He died in Austin on February 10, 1891---exactly ten years after the death of Elise.

In a sense, Lungkwitz's story is that of a broken dream. He came to Texas confident that he could make a lasting contribution to the art of the New World. During his lifetime, however, his work received little attention, even in Texas.

Lungkwitz might never have been widely recognized except for Dr. Samuel E. Gideon who, in 1918, discovered his sketches and paintings when he was doing research on early Texas artists. Writing in the *Magazine of Art*, he said:

"His Fredericksburg pictures show that he caught the spirit of the country, the intense blue of the Texas sky and the peaceful character of the bowl-shaped, flat-topped hills. He put all the majesty into the stately cypresses, into the twisted and gnarled live oak trees, and caught the color of the outcropping granite and sandstone boulders."

His principal biographer, the late James Patrick McGuire of the Institute of Texan Cultures, said that "collectively Lungkwitz presents a portrait of the Hill Country as it was in the early days...(His) art is a valuable legacy and will remain so for all who treasure the natural beauty of this section of Texas."

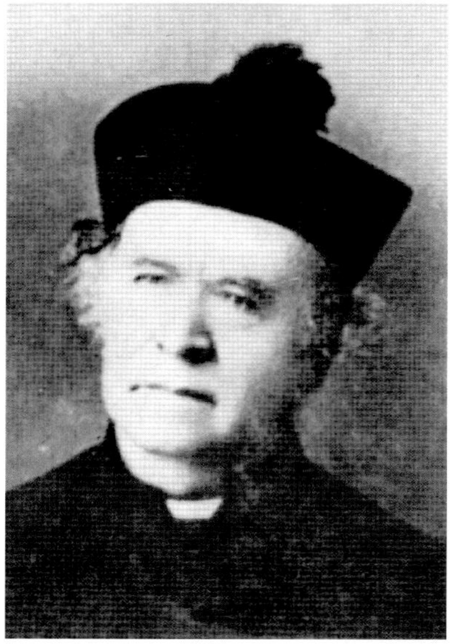

FATHER PETER TARRILLION
1821-1900
"Painter Priest"

Photo Courtesy of Gillespie County Historical Society, Inc.

As a youngster, Peter Tarrillion never thought of becoming an artist. He dreamed of a lifetime in the Church; yet he somehow felt that he lacked the ardor to become a parish priest.

He had no misgivings about his capabilities as a natural artisan, however. Born an only child in Edlingen, Lothringen, Germany, in 1821, he recognized this talent early on and developed himself as a locksmith, an organ and clock-maker and as a technician and craftsman in many fields. He saw in crafts an avenue for fulfilling his passionate longing for a lifetime of service to his fellow men, even though he resisted the dedication of his life to the priesthood.

Fate, as it often does in the lives of men, changed his plans. In 1852, he immigrated to the United States with a cousin, also named Peter Tarrillion. They settled in Pikesville, Missouri, and he entered a Missouri seminary. On March 25, 1855, he was ordained a priest at Galveston, Texas. The following December, he visited Fredericksburg, which had been settled less than nine years earlier. He found a Catholic congregation without a priest.

The parishioners liked the gentle, blonde, 5 foot, 10 inch priest and urged him to stay. He could not accept the invitation, but he returned the next year and spent the Spring and Summer. By then, however, he had been assigned to a parish in Colorado County.

Father Tarrillion had fallen in love with the Hill Country and hoped to return. The chance came almost 11 years later. In March, 1867, he became pastor of Fredericksburg's St. Mary's Catholic Church. He was to remain for 32 years.

Once Father Tarrillion had assumed the Fredericksburg parish, he became a hands-on artisan as well as a good shepherd to his flock. When a new parish house was built in 1868, he took an active role in both the planning and the construction. Five years later, when the former residence of the priest was converted into a parochial school, Father Tarrillion built the tower clock, three new bells and a new pipe organ.

While carrying out his priestly duties, he not only found time to mold the wax candles used in the Mass, but he made new candlesticks for the altar. As a glass blower, he shaped small birds to decorate the sanctuary. Father Tarrillion built a sundial for the parish yard and organized young men of the church into a band which he conducted himself. An expert in pyrotechnics, he made fireworks for church picnics and for special events like the dedication of Our Lady of the Lake College in San Antonio.

Father Tarrillion never considered himself an artist, but he picked up his easel when St. Mary's Church needed decoration and lacked the funds to buy traditional religious artifacts. He painted three canvases that are 56x34-inches in size, and are stretched on 2x4-inch pieces of wood. They still survive, although they are in poor

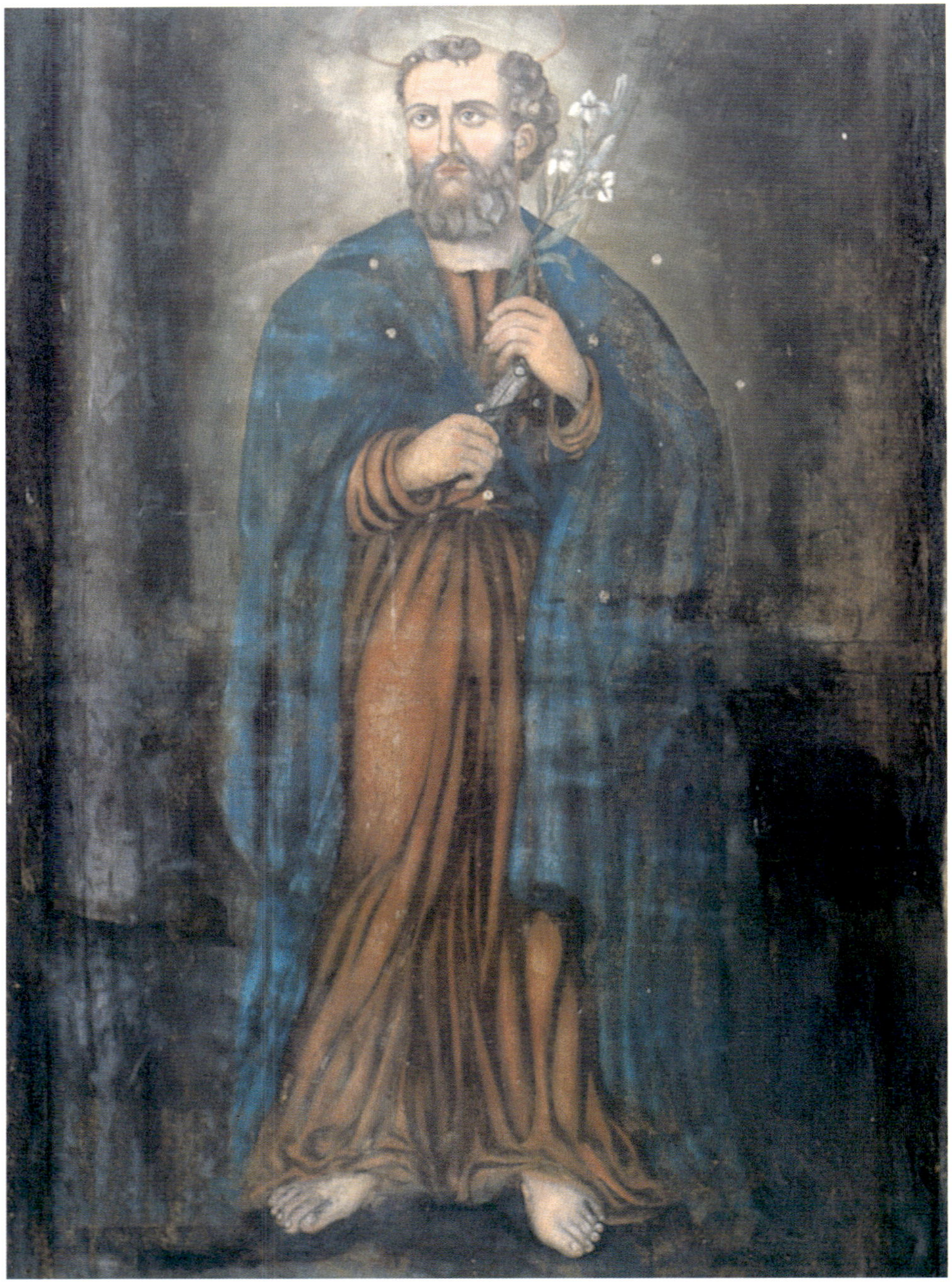

condition and no longer hang in the church.

Despite his many extracurricular activities, Father Tarrillion was a pious, zealous and much loved priest. In 1899, at the age of 78, his health began to fail. He resigned his parish and moved to San Antonio where he died March 25, 1900. He is buried in St. Joseph's Cemetery.

He remains, however, an almost legendary figure in the history of both religion and visual arts in Fredericksburg.

"ST. JOSEPH"
BY FATHER PETER TARRILLION
56" X 34" OIL
Collection of St. Mary's Catholic Church, Fredericksburg, Texas

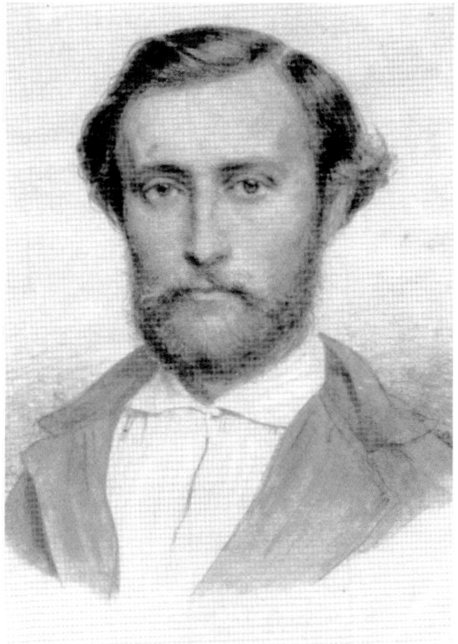

FRIEDRICH RICHARD PETRI
1824-1857
"Artist Historian"

FRIEDRICH RICHARD PETRI - SELF PORTRAIT
Courtesy of The Texas Memorial Museum, acc. #2269-5

Friedrich Richard Petri lived only a scant six years in Fredericksburg, but he managed to leave behind dozens of paintings, drawings and preliminary sketches recording the history of a community that was only five years old when he arrived.

He was, by any standards, a genius with his pencils, crayons, water colors and tempera. He rarely used oils, but when he did, the results were masterful. His talents were such that, at age 14, he was accepted at the *Akademie der Bildenden Kunste* (Royal Academy) in his native Dresden, Germany. Studying alongside some of the country's best artists, he won six awards of merit!

He even looked like an artist. He was of slight build, had grave blue eyes and expressive fingers that seemed to be made for work at the easel. And while he was plagued with bad health all of his short life---he had tuberculosis, augmented by malaria---he managed to produce a voluminous record of the people and places in the frontier German settlement where he had chosen to live out his days.

Petri was born July 31, 1824, the son of a master shoemaker in Dresden. Not much is known of his life before he enrolled at the Academy and met Hermann Lungkwitz, an older student who was a struggling self-taught artist. The two became close friends and later Lungkwitz would marry Petri's sister, Elisabet.

Germany at that time was in the midst of revolution. Their last year at the academy was anything but peaceful, although both Petri and Lungkwitz completed their studies. Later, however, both became involved in the political upheaval and took part in some of the street fighting. One of their comrades was the composer and poet, William Richard Wagner.

Meanwhile, both had continued to paint. Petri's early work was primarily of mythological and Biblical scenes. Portraiture and landscapes did not become his genre until he joined Lungkwitz and a group from both families in immigrating to the United States in 1851.

After a stop for several months in Wheeling, Virginia (now West Virginia), they moved on to Texas, settling first in New Braunfels and later moving to Fredericksburg. Here Lungkwitz and his wife (Petri's sister Elisabet) bought a 320-acre farm on Live Oak Creek. They were joined there by Petri and another sister, Marie; Lungkwitz's mother and his sister, Therese; and later by Lungkwitz's brother, Adolph.

Throughout the long journey from Germany to Wheeling and finally to Texas, Petri stayed busy making sketches and completed drawings. Sometimes he and Lungkwitz collaborated, with Petri doing the figures and his friend filling in the landscape. While every Texas scene seemed to attract Petri, it was the Indian that he favored.

He seemed to have a special knack for making friends with the tribes that lived in and around Fredericksburg, and he came to know well the Comanches,

Caddos and Lipan Apaches. He often gave them the sketches he made of them, cementing a bond of friendship. Once when a band of hostile Comanches threatened his cabin, he pacified them by setting up his easel and making a drawing of them.

Petri was not the first artist to use Texas Indians as subjects. Only a few years earlier, Seth Eastman, whose specialty was that of sketching Indians, had lived briefly in Fredericksburg. Eastman's goal was to paint the Indian in his habitat. Petri painted portraits of them and recorded their every day activities in his drawings.

Eastman, the soldier-artist, had been stationed at Fort Martin Scott and his paintings and drawings provide a valuable record of activities there. However, the historic frontier post also provided Petri with one of his best subjects.

His oil rendition of Fort Martin Scott, although unfinished, is an invaluable contribution to the history of the fort. In the painting, and in a more detailed pencil sketch, Petri captured life as it was lived daily. In addition to a defense, Martin Scott was an important trading post. Indians brought their buffalo skins and corn to exchange for beads and arms. Farmers bartered cotton and other crops for coffee, bacon and medicines. Petri captures these activities in his works.

Historians say that Petri's paintings are also important because they give visual support to the unusual and friendly relationship which existed between the Fredericksburg Germans and the Indian tribes.

That Petri was able to produce the number of drawings and paintings that he did is surprising in view of the shortage of artistic materials on the frontier. Both he and Lungkwitz had arrived from Germany with a large supply of paints, paper, canvas, brushes and pencils, but they were difficult and sometimes impossible to replace.

Lack of materials did not deter Petri. If there was no paper handy, he would sketch on the fly leaf of the nearest book. He even painted on the reverse side of the certificates he had received at the Royal Academy. Because paints were almost impossible to obtain even in Austin or San Antonio, he made most of his pigments out of the native clays in the area. He obtained them from friendly Indians, bribing them with trinkets.

Combining these home-made materials with his extraordinary talent, Petri left hundreds of sketches that excel in craftsmanship. From his arrival in the Hill Country, he was intrigued by the colorful dress of the Indians and their lifestyles. He captured much of this in his paintings. Unfortunately, some of his work done with these primitive substances has not survived.

However, most of his sketches and paintings of his close friends and relatives were preserved. He was close to the Lungkwitz "family" which, of course, included two of his sisters, Elisabet and Marie. Because he also lived in the Lungkwitz compound, he delighted in sketching members of the family. He produced oil

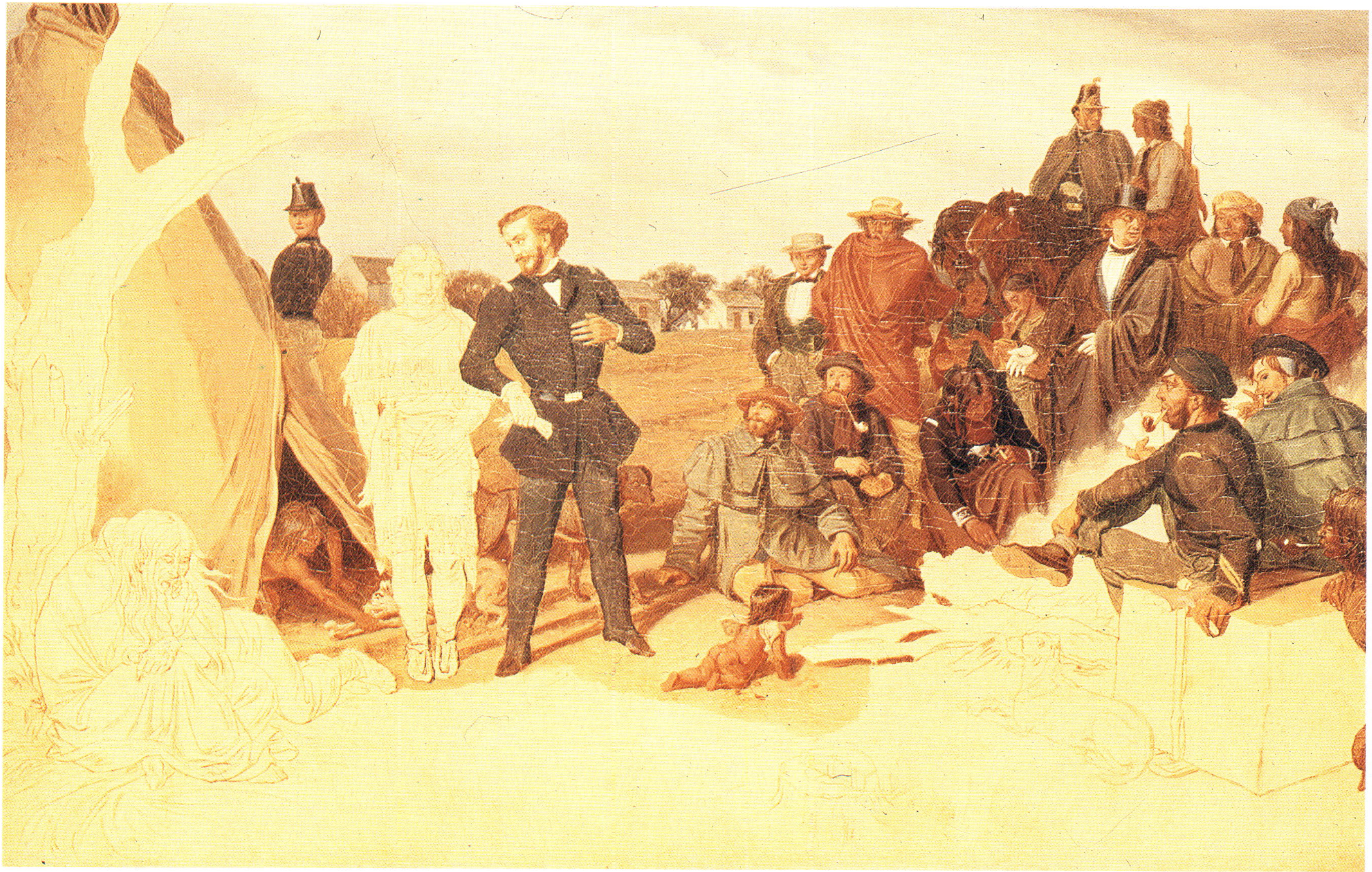

"FORT MARTIN SCOTT"
BY FRIEDRICH RICHARD PETRI
16 3/4" X 23 1/4" UNFINISHED OIL
Courtesy of the Texas Memorial Museum, acc. #2225

portraits of Hermann, Elisabet and Therese Lungkwitz. After his sister, Marie, married Jacob Kuechler, a Fredericksburg surveyor, he did an oil portrait of the couple as a gift.

His sketches in pencil and crayon of tiny Martha and Max Lungkwitz, his young niece and nephew, are almost camera-like in detail. Just before Petri's death in December, 1857, Elisabet gave birth to twin girls. One of his last sketches shows the parents ministering to the new arrivals.

Shortly after completing the sketch, Petri took to his bed with a high fever. While the other men were away working in their fields, he got up and wandered down to the Pedernales River, possibly hoping to cool the fever. He drowned and is buried on what was once the Lungkwitz farm.

The voluminous number of Petri's sketches and paintings are the only clues to the man and his times. He kept no diary and never bothered to keep any record of his work. None of his sketches and paintings are signed. If he wrote a single letter, researchers have not been able to find it.

His only legacy is his work. As Pauline Pinckney wrote in *Painting in Texas--The 19th Century* (1967: University of Texas Press, Austin):

"He possessed a greater native skill than many frontier artists of the American scene, and had he lived in another decade, he no doubt would have reached a place of eminence. So bound together were his talent, skill and enthusiasm that his work remains on the highest level."

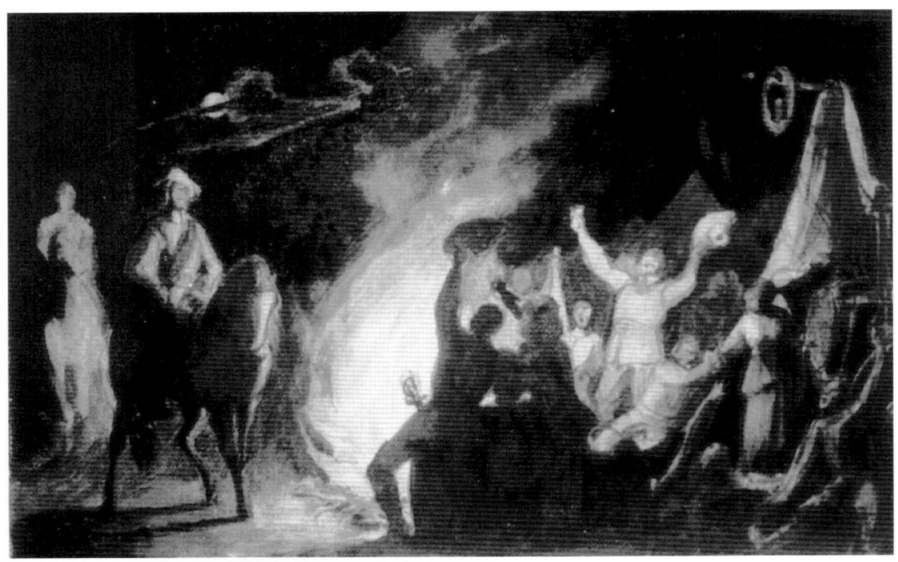

"CAMPFIRE SCENE"
BY FRIEDRICH RICHARD PETRI
7 1/2" X 10" WATERCOLOR AND INK
Courtesy of the Texas Memorial Museum, acc. #2316

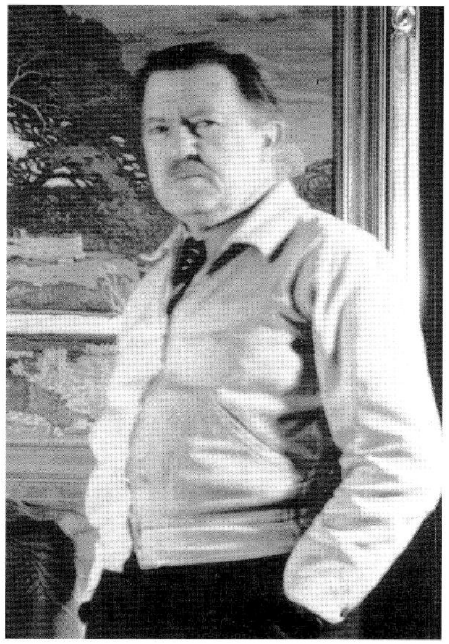

EDWARD G. EISENLOHR
1872-1961
"The Artist, Writer, Lecturer"

Photo Courtesy of Pioneer Memorial Library, Fredericksburg, Texas

Edward G. Eisenlohr was born in Cincinnati, Ohio, spent most of his professional life in Dallas, and never lived in the Texas Hill Country. It and Fredericksburg claimed him, however, because he sketched and painted here, and four of his works are displayed proudly in the Pioneer Memorial Library.

He considered himself a Texan by choice, and was closely tied to Texas by his own German heritage. His grandparents, the Rev. and Mrs. Christian Gustav Wilhelm Eisenlohr, and their son, Rudolph, had arrived here from the Black Forest in 1850 with the second wave of immigrants from Germany. Rev. Eisenlohr had accepted the pastorate of the First Protestant Church in Prince Carl's new settlement of New Braunfels.

The Eisenlohrs loved Texas, but it was short on educational facilities. In 1857, they moved to Cincinnati so Rudolph could study pharmacology. After a short stay there, the family went back to Germany so Rudolph could do advanced work in his chosen field. While there he met and married Emma Hellner, a promising young artist.

In 1870, the young couple returned to Cincinnati and Rudolph became a druggist. On November 9, 1872, their son, Edward, was born. Later they had a daughter, Valerie. Rudolph's business prospered, but he couldn't put aside the fond memories he had of being a youngster in New Braunfels. He moved the family to Texas, settling in Dallas. Edward and Valerie grew up there.

By the time Edward was ready for school, he was showing an interest in both art and literature. His mother had taught him how to draw simple pictures when he was barely old enough to walk. In school, he would draw sketches on the back of his textbooks. In his Physical Geography class, he illustrated his notebook with detailed pen and ink drawings.

When he was 14, he entered his first exhibition at the State Fair of Texas and won first prize with his drawing of a map of the State of Texas. He also began writing travel articles and short stories for magazines, and would continue to write and lecture throughout his life.

His father's business had prospered, and in 1887 the family moved to Germany for a few years so Edward could study art in Zurich and Karlsruhe.

When the Eisenlohrs returned to Dallas, Edward felt that he needed still more study. He took a job as a bank clerk---a position he held for 19 years---but he continued to paint and study under famous artists like Frank Reaugh and Robert Onderdonk. When one of his paintings was accepted for exhibit at the Cincinnati Art Museum, he took a leave of absence from the bank and went back to Europe for more instruction. He was 34 years old.

From that point on, art occupied all of his time. Using pencil, pen and ink, oils, pastels and lithography, he devoted the rest of his life to painting the

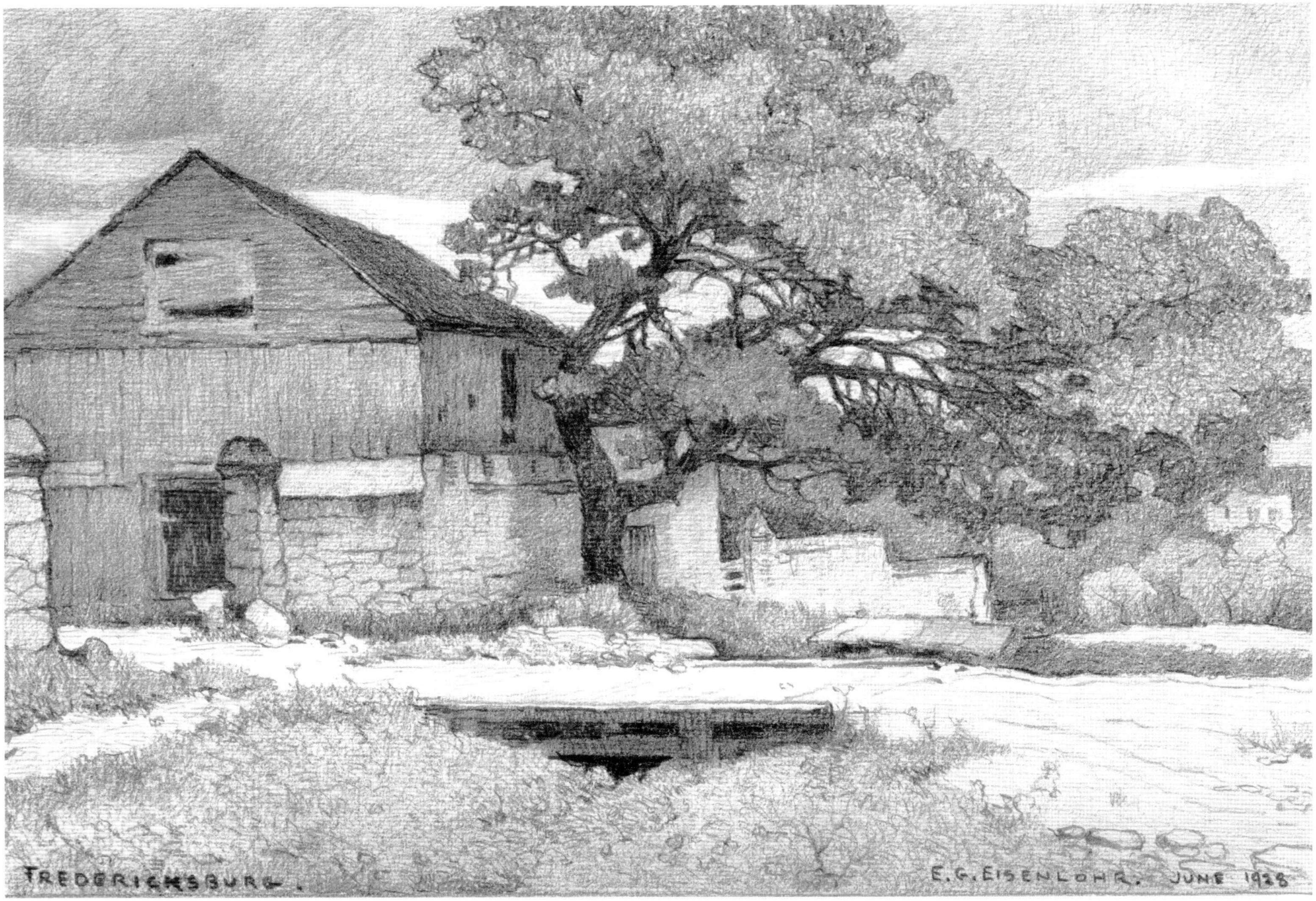

"GATEWAY AND BARN AT NIMITZ HOTEL"
BY EDWARD G. EISENLOHR
8 1/4" X 11 5/8" PENCIL-JUNE 29, 1928
Courtesy of the Gillespie County Commissioners Court and the McDermott Building Oversight Committee, Fredericksburg, Texas

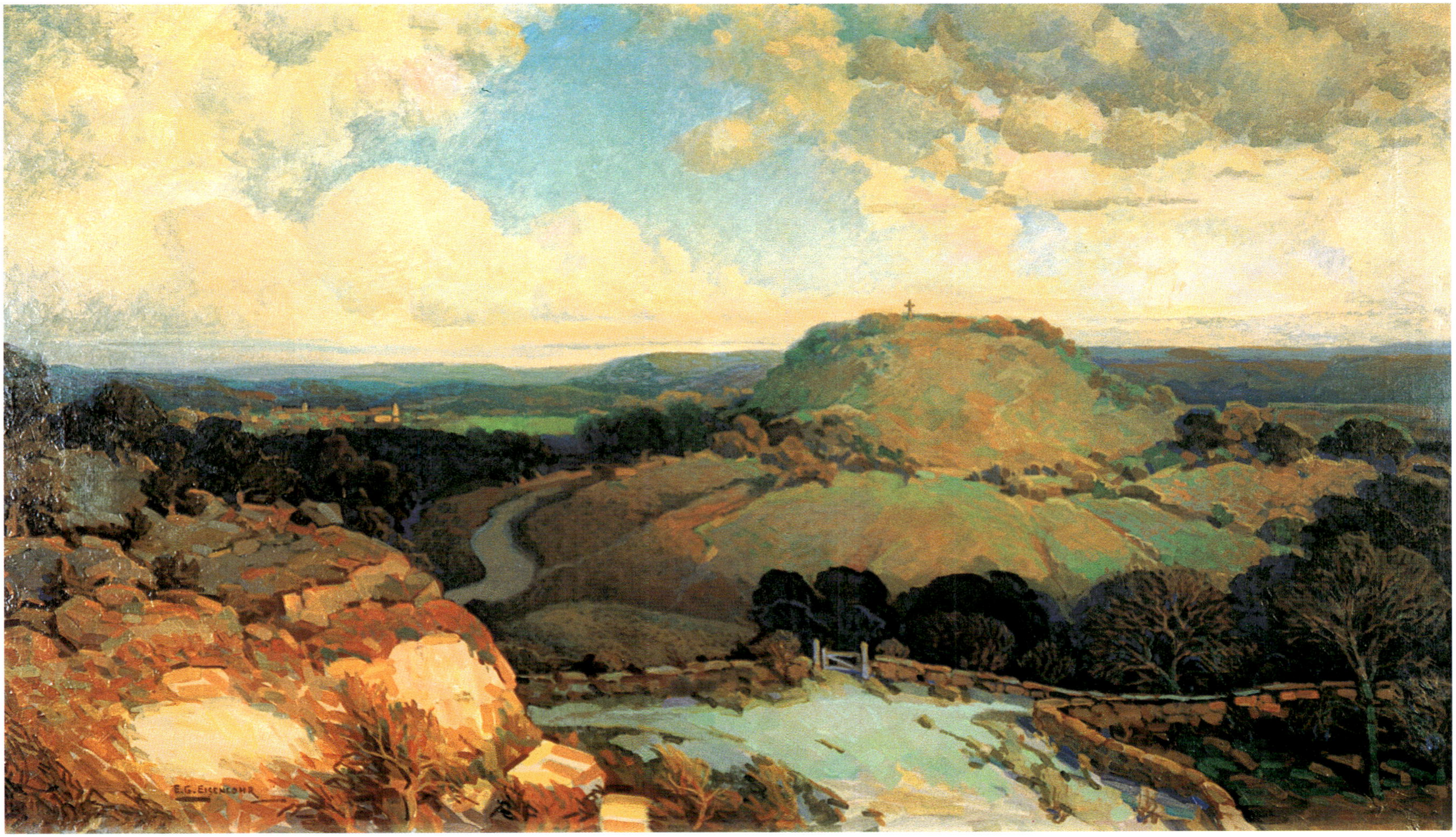

"THE CROSS OF THE PIONEERS"
BY EDWARD G. EISENLOHR
30" X 50" OIL
Courtesy of the Gillespie County Commissioners Court and the McDermott Building Oversight Committee, Fredericksburg, Texas

landscapes of the Southwest.

Although a 20th century artist, he has been called “one of the pioneer landscape painters of Texas.” In 1924, during a State Fair of Texas exhibit, his paintings were hung near those of Claude Monet, the French “father of impressionism.” Critics noted a striking similarity between their works---an unusual tribute to Eisenlohr.

Today Eisenlohr’s work hangs in museums in Austin, Dallas, New Orleans, San Antonio, Houston and elsewhere. One of his paintings and three sketches are in the Pioneer Memorial Library in Fredericksburg.

Fredericksburg always was one of his favorite places to visit. Unlike many other German settlements in Texas, the town has retained much of its Old World charm. Thus, it was the place where he could recapture a sense of his German heritage while enjoying and painting the beautiful scenery.

His painting in the Pioneer Memorial Library is a 30x50-inch oil titled “Cross of the Pioneers.” It depicts a cross, erected on a rounded hill north of Fredericksburg, believed to have been first put there in 1757 by Spanish padres in route to the San Saba de Santa Cruz Mission near the present town of Menard.

Beside it is the 10x12-inch original pencil sketch from which the oil was made. Both were gifts to the library by Edward Helmle and his sister, Gertrude, the nephew and niece of the artist.

Two other Eisenlohr sketches, gifts of Dr. and Mrs. P. O’B. Montgomery of Dallas and Fredericksburg, also hang in the library. One, “Gateway and Barn at Nimitz Hotel,” is dated June 28, 1928. The second, “Church Tower,” is a drawing of St. Mary’s Catholic Church and is dated June 29, 1928. The dates indicate that the artist drew them both on one of his visits to Fredericksburg.

From early childhood, Edward Eisenlohr had but one ambition. He wanted to be an artist and portray the Southwestern landscape in a significant way. He had fulfilled that ambition, and more, when he died in 1961. He is buried in Dallas.

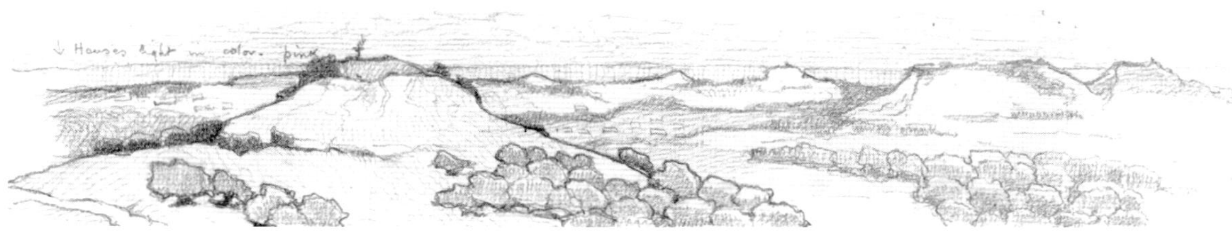

DETAIL FROM THE PENCIL DRAWING OF
“THE CROSS OF THE PIONEERS”
BY EDWARD G. EISENLOHR
10"X 14" PENCIL
Courtesy of the Gillespie County Commissioners Court and the McDermott Building Oversight Committee, Fredericksburg, Texas

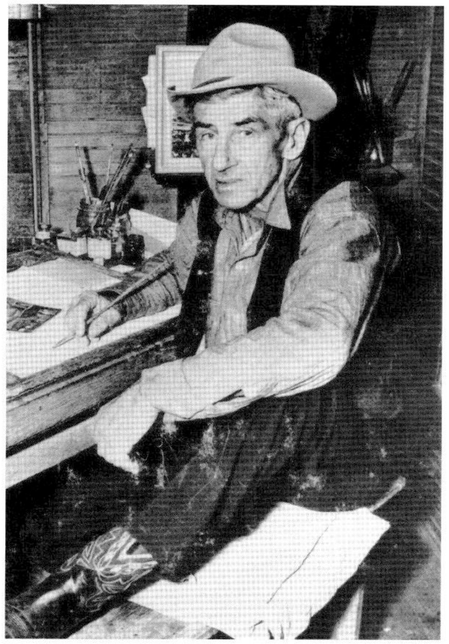

HAROLD OSMAN KELLY
"KELLY BLUE"
1884-1955
"The Primitive Who Was Different"

Photo from the Collection of Texas A&M University

Harold Osman Kelly was a mule-skinner, farmer, logger, bull-whacker, mill-hand, sheep-herder, freighter, rancher and sometime-artist.

He was 66 years old before he thought of painting as a serious avocation. His entire output would scarcely fill even a small gallery. Yet only three years after his work was exhibited for the first time, an art critic for *The American Weekly* called him "one of the Lone Star State's least-publicized natural wonders."

"Kelly Blue," the name he acquired because of the bright blue skies that became the trademark of his work, never lived in Fredericksburg. But he was a frequent visitor. He once told an interviewer that he had four loves: his wife, Jessie; polka music; Shiner keg beer, and Fredericksburg.

Kelly was born in Bucyrus, Ohio, in 1884, and grew up in a railroad family in Lancaster, Pennsylvania. A railroad career held no interest for him, however, and he left home early. He roamed the country, working in 30 different states and in almost as many occupations. Along the way, he met and married Jessie Bowers in Arkansas.

He had been introduced to Texas in 1905 when he stopped in for awhile to work as a cowboy. He liked the place and, in the early 1930's, settled on a farm near Texline in the Texas Panhandle just as the great drought began. After battling dust storms for five years, he and Jessie sold the land for what they could get and headed south.

By the time they reached Blanket (pop 390), in Brown County, their money was almost gone. However, they found a run-down place and settled in. He died there in December, 1955.

Kelly was born with a native talent for sketching. He admitted, however, that working with horses was his first love. He hadn't bothered with art until he moved to Blanket.

One Christmas, with the weather bad and time on his hands, he bought a set of water colors like those used to teach art in grade school. He painted a few Christmas cards and sent them to friends. Later he tried the technique on pieces of cardboard and finally on small squares of canvas.

Kelly's work might never have become known outside his circle of friends if it hadn't been for Lexie Dean Robertson. She was a poet who lived at Rising Star, a hamlet north of Blanket. She heard about the cowboy-painter and went to see him. His water colors impressed her and she persuaded him to switch to oils. Later she took some of his paintings in the new medium to Dallas for appraisal by experts. Kelly was an instant success.

Collectors like Stanley Marcus saw his pieces and began buying. Soon Kelly's works were being reproduced in magazines like *Life*, *Time*, *Flair* and others. In 1950, the Dallas Museum of fine Arts presented the first solo exhibition of Kelly's work. Of the 32 exhibited, 27 had to be borrowed from those who already had purchased them. The remaining five were snapped up the first day.

In 1960, Doubleday & Co., the New York publisher, brought out a book of his paintings and letters. In 1979, Texas A&M University Press published *Kelly Blue* by William W. Johnson. It is a biography of the artist and includes the paintings and letters from the original book. Kelly's letters to the Johnsons and six of his paintings are permanently housed at A&M.

The late Frank Wardlaw, then director of the Texas A&M Press, called Kelly "one of the few really important primitive artists this region has ever produced." Kelly also called his work "primitive," but he disliked being compared to Grandma Moses.

He took some pride, however, in the fact that his painting was done under circumstances that any other artist would consider primitive if not intolerable. His "studio" was the front room of his ramshackle frame home. His easel was a battered desk where he could sit on a high bench and look out of a window, which was kept spotlessly clean. The house had no electricity and his only light, except for that which came through the window, was the glow of a kerosene lamp. He rarely turned out more than one small painting a month.

Kelly preferred a small canvas and he used every inch, which was a bane to framers. He was meticulous, slow and often used the dry brush technique for his water colors. He disdained a palette, even after switching to oils, preferring to keep his paints in a water color tray.

When at work, he smoked one hand-rolled cigarette after another, often dropping ashes into the fresh oil. It is said that an "authentic" Kelly Blue painting always has some bits of ashes and tobacco embedded in it.

His technique was simple. He always painted the sky or background first, then the foreground. He painted the human figures nude, dressing them later.

Kelly loved Hill Country scenes. He visited Fredericksburg often, staying at the old Nimitz when it still operated as a hotel. Anytime he learned that an oom-pah band was going to be playing polkas for dancing, he headed toward Fredericksburg.

He especially loved the polka. It seemed to get him in the mood to paint. He often played old polka recordings on his ancient phonograph while he was working. If ladies were present, he would lay aside his brush and ask them to dance. However, he loved the town of Fredericksburg even more than its music.

Kelly described a perfect weekend in Fredericksburg this way:

"A few glasses of good keg beer on Saturday night, a few nice waltzes, church on Sunday morning and watching the quarter horses dust out in the afternoon.

"The Hill Country rests me, and I have the same feeling in Fredericksburg

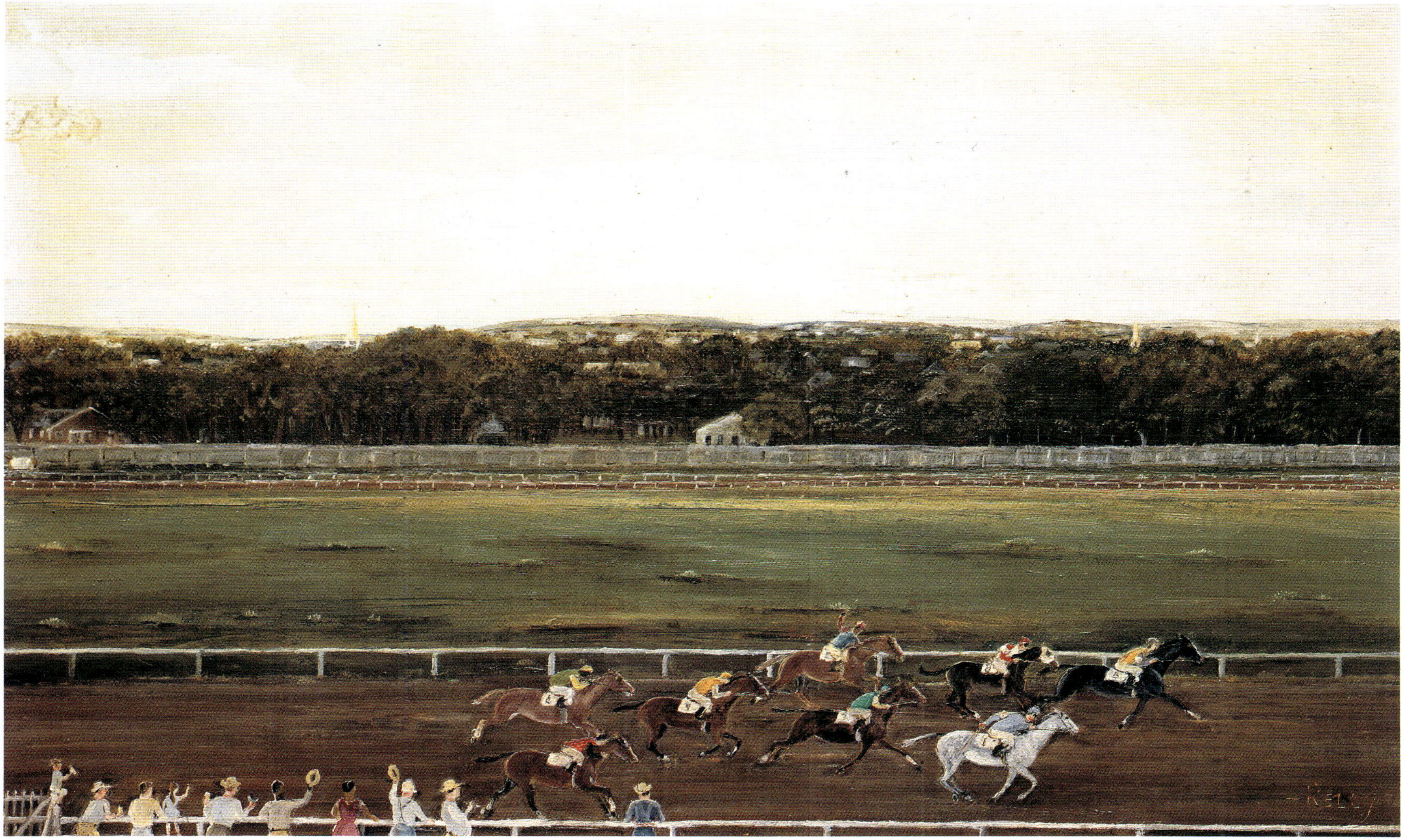

"FOURTH OF JULY RACES"
BY HAROLD OSMAN KELLY "KELLY BLUE"
8 1/4" X 13 1/2" OIL ON BOARD
From the Collection of Texas A&M University

that I had in the Ohio town of my nativity," he said. "No rush, no push, just good people going about their affairs, their work and play, in a pleasant manner."

He loved to write letters. Although he was self-taught as an artist and had little education of any kind, he could be erudite when it came to writing. His words also could be as primitive and direct as his painting. In one letter he tells of a visit from a lady painter whom he describes as "the pansy and bluebonnet variety."

"...She told me of the instructors she had studied under, that my picture was not correctly proportional, how she was taught to see the way to paint by Professor Whoozis, who is a Christian Scientist,...(asked) why I didn't copy Currier & Ives prints, etc. By the time I was ready to tell her that I didn't give a grandmother's damn how she painted...I saw she didn't know her ass from a Confederate bit and bid her goodbye."

One of his favorite paintings of Fredericksburg was titled "October-First Monday," then a regular trades day when farmers from all around came to town. As one critic said of this work:

"As in many of Kelly's paintings, this one incorporates the best of all villages and towns that he has visited and captured in his mind. He very much admired the neat orderliness....the sturdiness of Fredericksburg, Texas, with its clean native stone homes, barns and outbuildings was to become almost an obsession."

Kelly did not depend on photographs or preliminary sketches for his work. He painted from memory. When he used human figures at all, he kept them minute. But as one critic has said:

"In all his work you have a feeling of camaraderie among the folk who are depicted. In his life, the kindness of friends and neighbors was to have a great impact."

This was especially true of those with whom Kelly Blue drank beer, listened to polkas and traded stories during his visits to Fredericksburg.

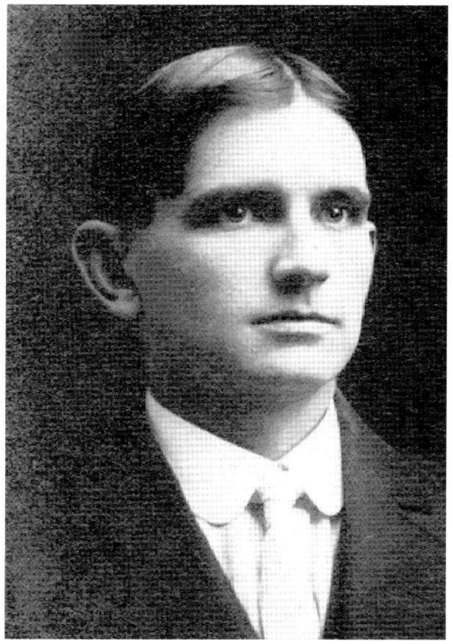

FELIX WEINHEIMER
1885-1955
"The Community Artist"

Photo Courtesy of
Yvonne Weinheimer Hartmann

Felix Weinheimer was a man of many talents.

He was a farmer, merchant, photographer, self-taught musician and, for 12 years, the postmaster of Stonewall.

He also was a self-taught artist. Much of his art work was done as his contribution to community projects. At least two of his paintings, however, are "primitives," showing how Fredericksburg's Main Street looked before it was paved, when horses were the principal mode of transport.

Felix was born in Stonewall on January 16, 1885, to a family that had come to Gillespie County with John O. Meusebach's settlers. He attended school there except for a year when he enrolled at St. Mary's Catholic School in Fredericksburg for religious instruction.

In 1909 he married Lydia Schmidt, and the couple spent their entire life in Stonewall. They had three children, two boys and a girl.

Like most of the German immigrants, his parents, Jacob and Johanne Bock Weinheimer, were farmers. Felix and a relative started Weinheimer and Company, a general merchandise store, on what is now Ranch Road One, the main road through Stonewall at that time. Eventually he owned two farms in the Stonewall area, one of which is still in the family. The other is where the Grape Creek Vineyard is now located.

Felix loved music. He played a coronet in the Stonewall community band, taught himself to play the violin and was accompanist for a singing group. Scenery for the Stonewall Auxiliary Club theatricals was usually painted by Felix, as were backdrops for the Stonewall Community Club displays at the annual Fair.

He did not restrict his art to that created at his easel. For the background of a display at the local fair one year, Felix created a picture of a red and white Hereford calf---made with red and white corn!

Painting was a hobby and so was photography, and many of Weinheimer's paintings were done from photos he had made. His "studio" was his home, where he worked in a favorite spot by a window. He had no particular routine, painting in his spare time. He hand-made most of the frames for his paintings.

The two views Weinheimer painted of Main Street were done as a part of the celebration of Fredericksburg's 100th anniversary in 1946. One looking east and the other west on Main Street, they are a lasting record of how the community looked a short time after Meusebach and his immigrants made their way here from Indianola in 1846.

Felix died August 8, 1955, and he and Lydia are buried in Fredericksburg in *Der Friedhof* cemetery.

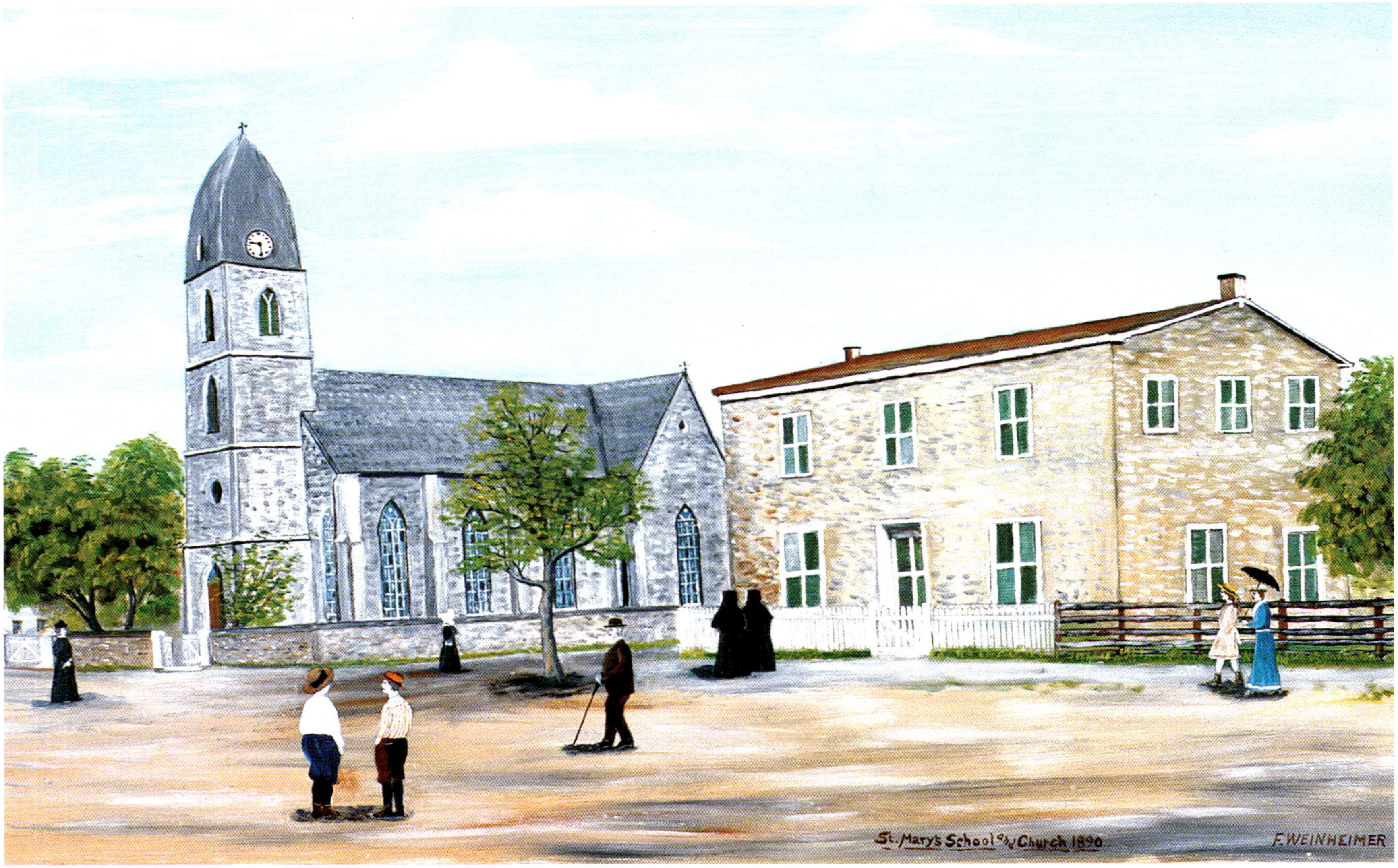

"ST. MARY'S SCHOOL AND CHURCH, 1890"
BY FELIX WEINHEIMER
15 1/4" X 24" OIL
From the Collection of
Knopp and Metzger, Inc.,
Fredericksburg, Texas

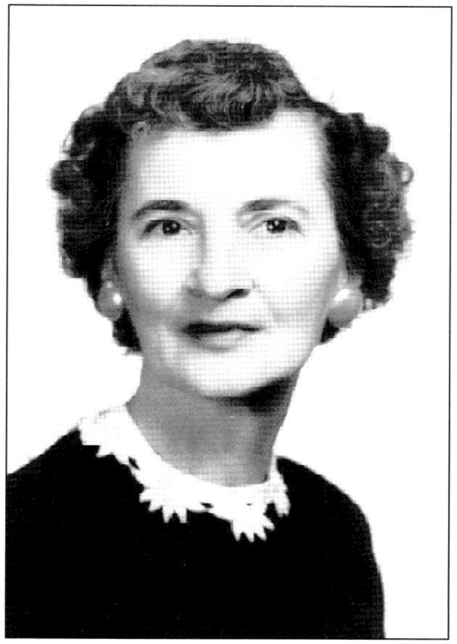

EDWINA MINTEL
1896-1966
"The Bluebonnet Artist"

Photo Courtesy of Helen Mintel Michaels

Edwina Mintel was born in San Antonio and died there, but Fredericksburg also was her home and studio for many years.

She loved painting and teaching, but these invariably took a back seat to her love for her three grandchildren. More than a half-century later, they still recall and recount their visits to "grandmother's and papa's farm."

She also was a writer---but only for her grandchildren. She wrote stories for them---tales about the farm and the wild animals that sometimes visited it---and illustrated them with her drawings and water colors. They remain unpublished family treasures.

Like many other artists, Edwina began drawing pictures as a child. Later she would study with painters like R.J. Onderdonk, Peter Hohenstedt, John Philipponi, José Arpa and Rolla Taylor.

Bluebonnets were one of her favorite subjects---so much so that she gave that name to the art school she operated in San Antonio in the 1920's and 1930's. While she was busy teaching and painting, her husband, Otto, operated Mintel Electric Co. in that city.

In the early 1940's, the Mintels decided to take things a little easier and bought a 360-acre farm north of Fredericksburg near Bear Mountain. They also opened a gift shop and electric lighting store in the 400 block of West Main Street. She continued to teach art, using a room in the southeast corner of the old courthouse building that now houses the Pioneer Memorial Library. Her lessons were free!

Although she weighed only 98 pounds, Edwina was a bundle of energy. She organized and was the first president of the Fredericksburg Art Club and was active in the Zonta Club. She loved to entertain and was known for her informal dinners. When she wasn't teaching or at her easel, she made cottage cheese for her friends.

Using oils, water color and pencil, she produced an enormous number of landscapes and still lifes. At one show in a San Antonio shopping center, 50 of her works were exhibited. She promoted some of the first outdoor art shows ever seen in San Antonio.

Edwina was never afraid to try something different. Once she painted designs in oil on some of her evening clothes. Others saw them and began asking her to paint theirs. In her home, she decorated her bathroom walls with paintings of her beloved bluebonnets.

Much as the Mintels loved Fredericksburg, running a dairy farm and caring for a herd of Guernsey cows proved to be too demanding. Milking and servicing cows, finding and keeping competent help, and getting the product to market while operating their business downtown left them little time for the activities they enjoyed. They sold the farm and, reluctantly, went back to the city.

She died there July 28, 1966.

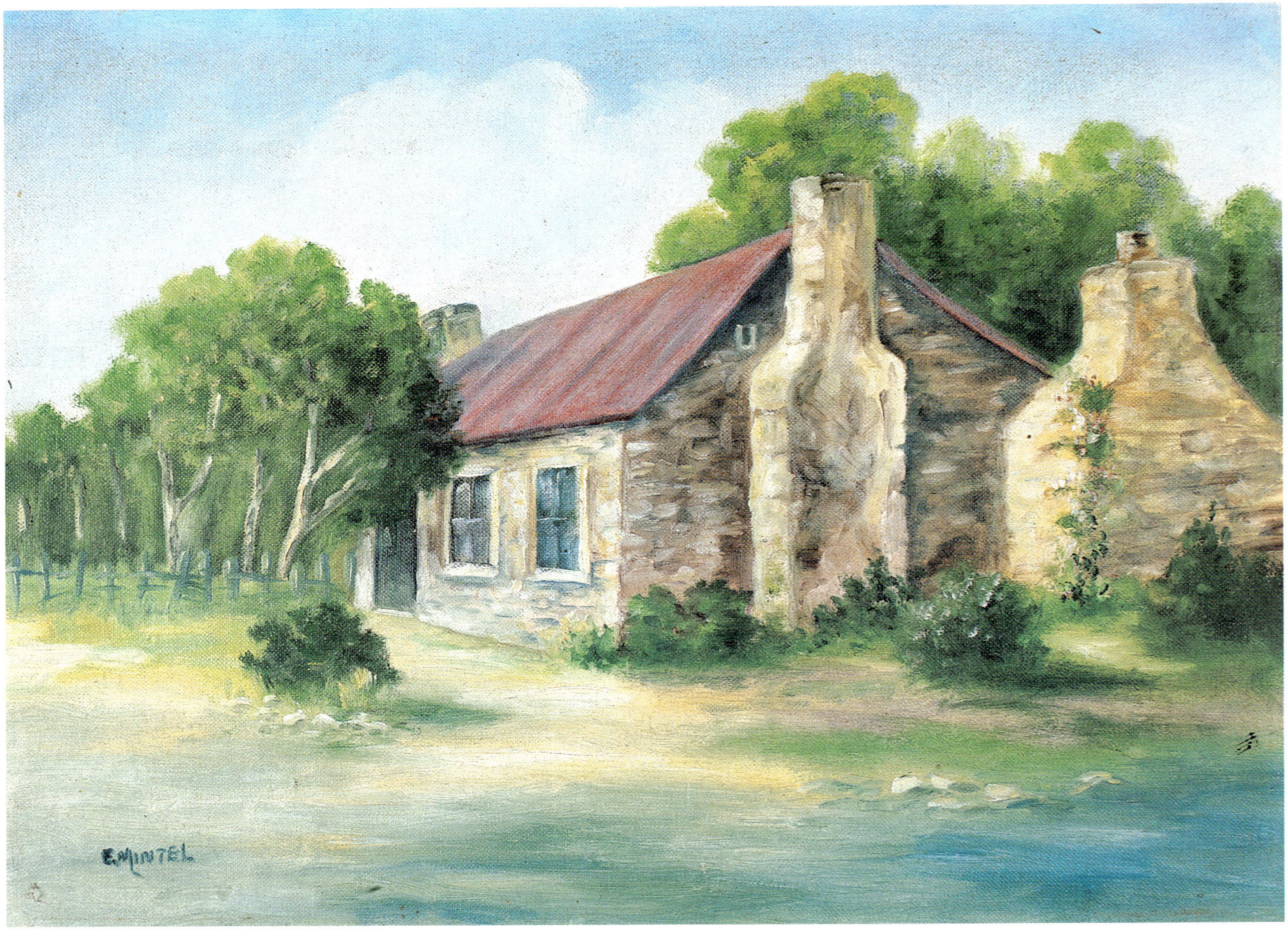

UNTITLED (PETER TATSCH HAUS)
BY EDWINA MINTEL
12" X 16" OIL
From the Collection of Mr. and Mrs. Glen Treibs

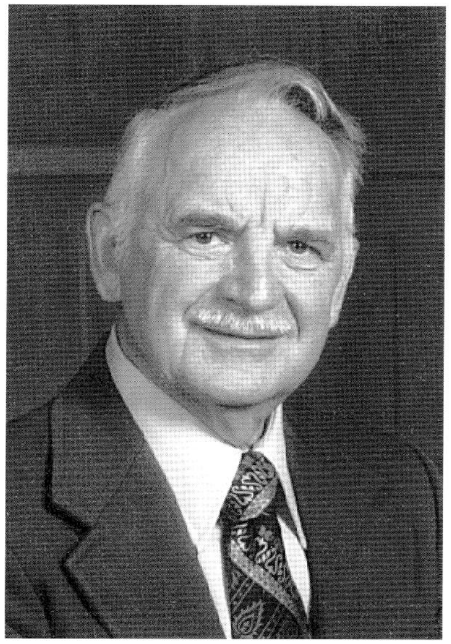

NORBERT CZARNOWSKI
1897-1994
"The Commercial Artist"

Photo From a Private Collection

He always insisted that he was a "commercial" artist---that the fine paintings and sketches he did were for his own personal pleasure. Yet when he died at age 96, his work had been shown in top exhibitions, and many of his paintings are in private and museum collections around the world today.

Norbert Czarnowski was born August 9, 1897, near Dansk, Poland. He came to the United States with his parents when he was 16. He planned to remain here the rest of his life, but when his native land was threatened by war, he went back to Poland and enlisted in the army, serving in France and Russia. His poignant sketches from World War I are in the permanent collection at the Polish Catholic Museum in Chicago.

After the Armistice, Norbert returned to America bent on a career as an artist. He enrolled in the Chicago Art Institute and later the Chicago Academy of Fine Arts. His work was good enough to be exhibited at the 1933 World Fair in Chicago. In 1937, he won a scholarship to the Warsaw University Art Institute and went back to Poland for a short time. When he completed studies with some famous European artists, he returned to America.

War clouds were gathering again, however, and soon Czarnowski found himself in the U.S. Army. This stint in the military steered him toward commercial art, as he was assigned to the Signal Corps Photo Unit and sent to Hollywood to work on propaganda films at Paramount Studios. When he was released from the Army, he was ready for a try at selling his talents in the business world.

For the next several years, Czarnowski had a variety of assignments. He was a draftsman and illustrator for businesses that included railroads, merchandising, heavy machinery, jewelry and pre-fabricated homes manufacturing. In Detroit, he designed ads and brochures for an automobile company.

However, while he was doing commercial art, he also was doing some oils and water colors for his own creative fulfillment. Norbert married Wanda Mary Pazdro in 1946, and was trying to find his niche in the art world. He had exhibited in several galleries in Chicago by the time he retired from commercial art in 1965. Then, with Wanda, he took time to travel the world looking for subjects that inspired him. They toured the Caribbean, Mexico, France, Spain, Germany, Africa and most of the United States.

After Wanda Mary's death on November 24, 1968, Norbert made a trip to Fredericksburg. His brother, Bogdan, and his wife, Charlotte, had a ranch here, and Norbert became enchanted with the German architecture and the hill country, and decided to make his home here someday.

Norbert moved to Texas soon after his visit. He established a studio in a reconverted barn on his brother's ranch. He began to paint in earnest.

One of his first contributions to his new home town was to design the original official crest of Fredericksburg. He painted the Old Steamboat Nimitz Hotel as it

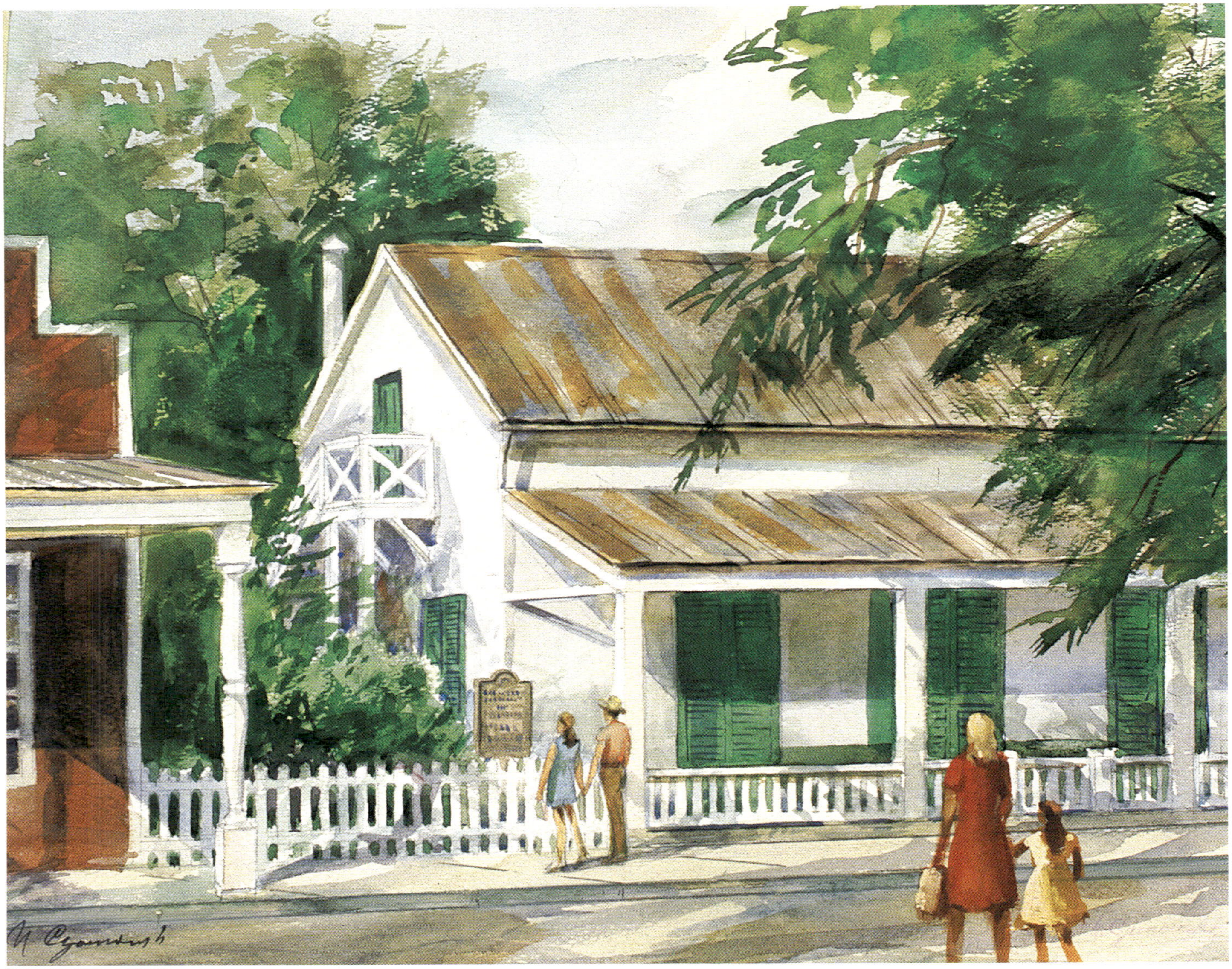

"NIMITZ BIRTHPLACE"
BY NORBERT CZARNOWSKI
14 3/4" X 19 3/4" WATERCOLOR
From a Private Collection

looked before it was remodeled into the Admiral Nimitz Museum in honor of the town's native son who made World War II history. Soon he was at work capturing other historic structures, portraits of local people and Hill Country landscapes.

Czarnowski had a special appreciation for abstract art and the latest developments, ideas and techniques. He felt that there were unexplored areas in the realistic approach to a subject. As a result, he was rarely satisfied with his work, often redoing a painting three or four times before it pleased him.

He also believed that producing a good work required the best materials. He imported his paper from France; his Windsor Newton colors from England; his brushes from Germany and his frames from Mexico.

Perhaps because he insisted on applying his talents to only the best subjects and used only the best quality materials, his work became known nationally. His portraits in both oil and water color attracted notice, as did his excellent landscapes. Soon the "commercial artist" was being exhibited in the best museums, ranging from the Togo Museum in Japan to others in Milwaukee, Detroit, San Antonio and elsewhere.

Galleries sought his work. For a time, Sears, Roebuck and Company operated art galleries in some of its major stores in an experiment suggested by the late actor and art connoisseur, Vincent Price. Czarnowski was among the artists included. Later a Sears executive wrote Norbert to tell him that he was "the most popular artist" among those whose works were shown.

Czarnowski talked often about his work.

"I don't use a special technique," he said. "I just paint from life, the way I see it. I prefer to paint with watercolor because it doesn't smear and you don't have to wait long for it to dry."

He looked first for good composition and didn't hesitate to make changes if Mother Nature didn't please him.

"The artist sometimes has to move things around in a scene to make a pretty picture. Composition is the most important part of painting. It's like setting a stage---putting things in the right place."

At age 95, and a patient in the Kerrville Veterans Administration Hospital's nursing facility, Czarnowski continued to paint. He constantly sketched or painted portraits of his doctors, nurses, other patients and visitors.

"I am so fortunate," he told an interviewer. "I am 95 and I can still walk on my own and I'm full of vigor. I think that's pretty good since most of the people here are bed-ridden or can't recognize their loved ones, and they're only in their eighties."

The vigor finally came to an end less than a month before his 97th birthday. He died July 10, 1994. He is buried in St. Mary's Cemetery in Fredericksburg, the home town he adopted 23 years before and where he spent "the happiest period of my life."

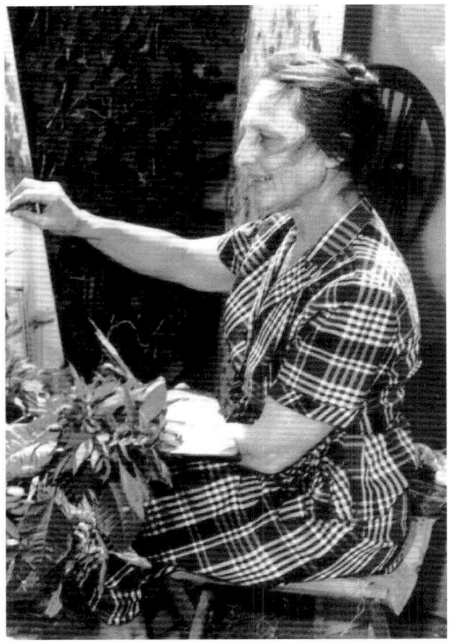

LYNE K. LEWIS HARPER
1897-
"The Town Founders' Artist"

Photo Courtesy of Fredericksburg Standard Radio Post

Two factors influenced Lyne Klingelhoefer Lewis Harper to devote much of her artistic talent to preserving the heritage of Fredericksburg.

First, she was born July 9, 1897 in the oldest house still standing in Fredericksburg. It was built by her grandfather, John J. Klingelhoefer, in 1847, a year after he and other German immigrants arrived to start a new settlement in "God's hills."

Second, her maternal grandfather was Johann Peter Tatsch, the noted furniture maker, who, in 1852, built another home that is still a Fredericksburg showplace. It attracts visitors from all over who marvel at its unique architecture, its huge chimney and a fireplace with an open hearth that is ten feet wide.

She has always been proud that she is the third generation of those who left Germany 150 years ago to build a new life in a strange land. And because she has been an artist for as long as she can remember, Mrs. Harper has deliberately used her innate abilities to preserve that heritage for generations still to come.

Lyne graduated from Fredericksburg High School in 1916, salutatorian of her class. Then she was off to Austin to become the first woman ever to study architecture and drawing at The University of Texas. She didn't graduate, but continued to take correspondence courses while teaching art, German and penmanship in Seguin public schools. She was awarded a lifetime teaching certificate by the State of Texas.

Later she was librarian for the schools in Seguin and coached the girls' basketball team. In her spare time, she took her first formal lessons in oil and china painting. Her teacher was Mrs. Joe F. Saegert, wife of the superintendent of schools.

With this as a start, Lyne went on to perfect her natural gift for painting. Through the years, she studied under José Arpa and Harold Roney in San Antonio; Peter Hohenstedt in Comfort and T.S. Cunningham, a former Fredericksburg resident. She went to workshops in Ruidoso and Cloudcroft, New Mexico, where Frederick Taubes taught her techniques of showing light in her paintings. From Samuel E. Gideon, she learned the mysteries of water color.

On October 8, 1929, she married Henry Welge Lewis, an independent oil operator who liked art and encouraged her to paint. Often when she had gone out to the countryside to work on one of her landscapes, Henry would have the evening meal ready when she returned.

Lyne and Henry lived in the Old Klingelhoefer home, at the corner of West Main and Acorn Street, with her mother, Sophie Tatsch Klingelhoefer. Lyne did substitute teaching in the Fredericksburg schools and gave private art lessons.

Henry's death in 1962 did not deter her from the goal of capturing the beauty of her native environment on canvas. She painted the native flowers, the beautiful old homes and the historic sites. She knew local history because she was a part of

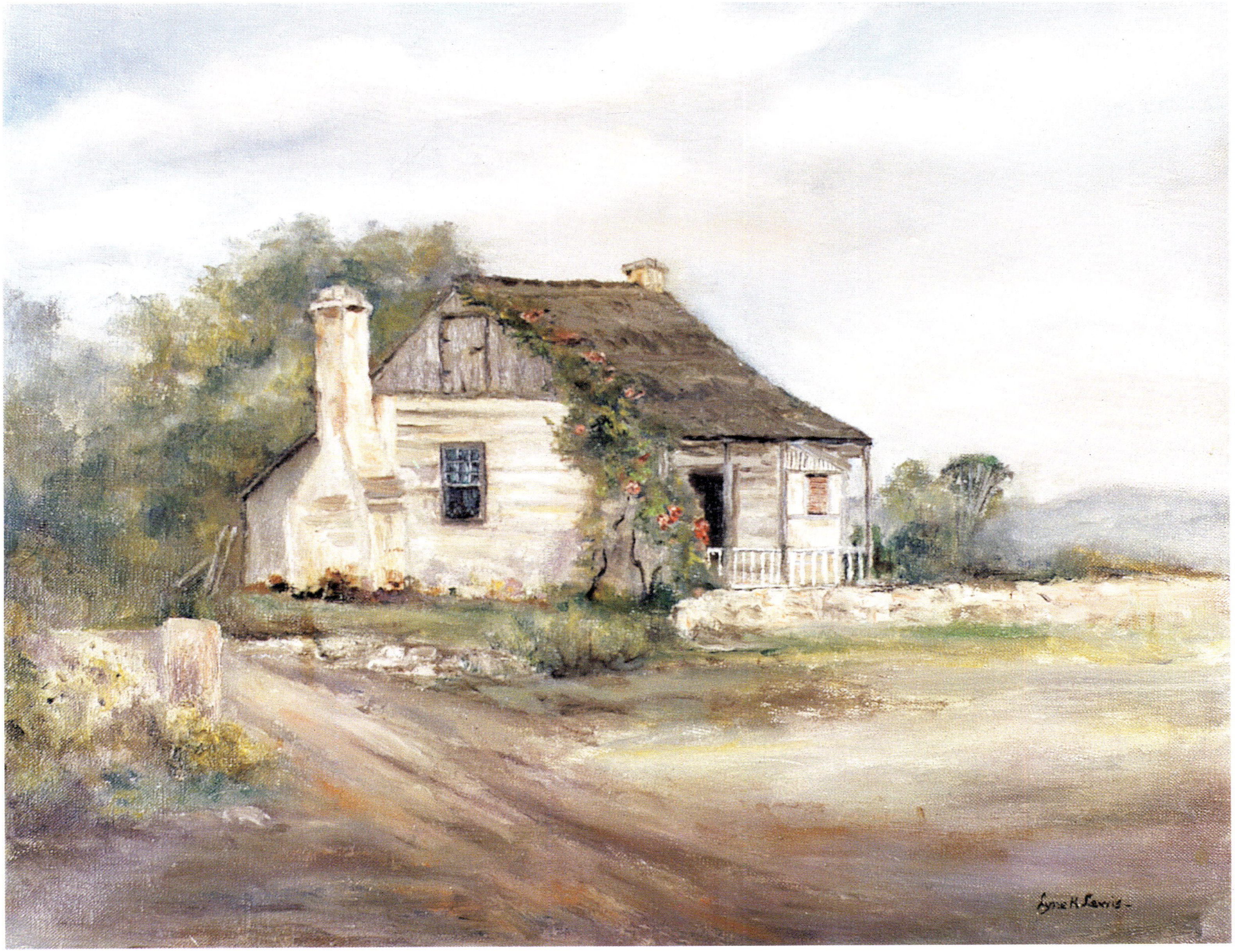

UNTITLED (LOEFFLER-WEBER HOUSE)
BY LYNE K. LEWIS HARPER
16" X 20" OIL ON CANVAS
From the Collection of
Mr. and Mrs. Mark Langerhans

so much of it, and she was dedicated to preserving that history in her work.

She accomplished this in unique ways. In 1947, when the need arose for an appropriate souvenir for the famed Easter Fires Pageant, she designed a plate which is still sold. When the Zion Lutheran Church, where she has worshipped for many years, celebrated its centennial, she designed a commemorative plate for the congregation. Always ecumenical, however, she painted a huge baptistry scene for the First Baptist Church when it was completed in 1955.

In 1970, Lyne married J. Watson Harper, a telephone engineer from Illinois. He died in 1985.

History, of course, has been her special love, second only to painting. She is a founding member of the Gillespie County Historical Society. In 1953, she was active in making the organization's first antique show a success. She has cataloged many books, antiques and other items of Fredericksburg's history for the Pioneer Museum, and was involved in the effort to preserve many of the town's unique structures, including the Nimitz Hotel.

Mrs. Harper has never stopped teaching, probably because she is convinced that "one can always learn, one is never finished." Throughout the years, aspiring artists and amateurs have come to her for advice and help and still do. At age 98, she still inspires Girl Scouts to study for their merit badge in art. Her philosophy is that training should never end, because study is equally important with experience and observation for success in art.

For her own teaching, Lyne has been awarded lifetime membership in Delta Kappa Gamma, an honorary organization for outstanding teachers. One of her proudest moments came when the DKG hung one of her paintings, a Hill Country bluebonnet scene, in its national headquarters offices in Austin.

She also has been a member for years of the prestigious Coppini Academy of Fine Arts in San Antonio and other art groups, and has had her work exhibited at the Elisabet Ney Museum of Art in Austin.

What inspired Lyne Klingelhoefer Lewis Harper to become an artist?

"I paint because I feel I have to," she says.

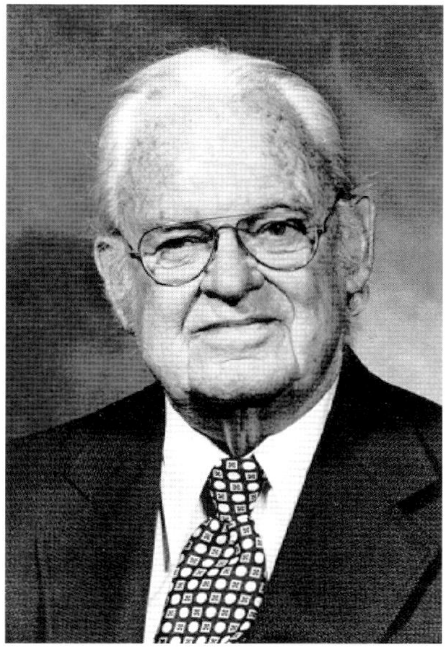

EDWARD MUEGGE SCHIWETZ
"BUCK"
1898-1984
"The Regional Artist"

Photo from the Collection of Texas A&M University

Edward Muegge Schiwetz was, by gubernatorial proclamation, "Dean of Texas Artists." The same document admonished Texans to consider him their "most beloved artist" because he used his unique talents to show his own love for his native state.

That affection shines through in the hundreds of pencil sketches, etchings and paintings of Texas landscapes, historic buildings, birds, animals and even industries that he produced over seven decades at his easel and drawing board.

Ecumenical in his choice of subjects, Schiwetz captured diverse Texas scenes ranging from off-shore drilling rigs in the Gulf, cathedrals in San Antonio, a barbecue stand in Cuero to his ever-present birds flying over rivers and lakes. Several of his more than 500 drawings and paintings were scenes of Fredericksburg and Gillespie County.

Three of these are reproduced in *Buck Schiwetz' Texas*, published in 1960 by The University of Texas Press. They are drawings of Lange's Mill at Doss; the John Dietrich Eckert house on Bear Creek between Fredericksburg and Comfort, and a Fredericksburg street scene showing two Catholic churches and an old home. They were done in 1926.

Schiwetz was born August 24, 1898 in Cuero, in South Central Texas, the eldest child of Berthold and Anna Reiffert Schiwetz, second generation German immigrants. As a child, he was nicknamed "Buckshot" by an uncle, then mayor of Cuero, and the appellation stuck.

Buck inherited the characteristic Teutonic sense of history and love of the soil from his parents. His artistic bent came from his mother. She laid aside her own considerable talent as a pencil artist to care for her first son, plus three more boys and a daughter who would follow.

By the time he was eight, she had recognized Buck's latent talent and set aside a room where he could draw to his heart's content. He was 12 when he painted his first credible watercolor---a Texas woodland scene with a cabin in the background. It would still be included in his exhibitions when he was in his eighties.

The elder Schiwetz was a banker who had no interest in art and sent his son to Texas A&M to become an electrical engineer. Buck was a miserable student. Instead of using his weekends to study, he hopped freight trains for Dallas or Houston and sketched buildings. School officials gave him a choice--flunk out or change his major. He switched to architecture and graduated with honors in 1921.

An offer from an architectural firm took him to Dallas. There he met Ruby Lee Sanders, a ceramic artist, and married her in 1926. They decided to head for the big time in New York.

The going was tough for awhile. Then a leading arts magazine began to accept his work. Officials at New York University saw it in print and offered him a teaching job. However, both he and Ruby Lee were homesick for Texas, and in 1929, they came to Houston. They arrived with 30 cents between them.

With a good record in New York behind him, Buck began to free-lance his work. An advertising agency, whose major client was the Humble Oil and Refining Company, hired him full-time as an illustrator. Eventually Buck would become a full partner in the agency and a close friend to the oil company's top officials.

In 1945, Humble started a publication called *The Humble Way*. It was a new idea in corporate journalism, aimed at demonstrating Humble's leadership in the petroleum industry to their stockholders and customers. The emphasis would be on Texas and its heritage before, and after, oil was discovered. To accomplish this, they hired the best writers and the best artists to illustrate their material. They asked Buck Schiwetz to illustrate the first issue.

That issue would launch *The Humble Way* as a classic among business publications, and make Buck Schiwetz one of the best-known artists in the Southwest. He was given carte blanche authority to travel Texas and capture the heritage of the state by drawing or painting ranch scenes, hills and lakes, crumbling old Army forts, courthouses, the unique homes built by early settlers from other countries---anything that would show the reader the soul of Texas.

After several issues, *The Humble Way* had attracted reader attention not only in the United States, but around the world. Editor Walter Beach, who shared Buck's love of Texas, decided to combine a number of these beautifully illustrated articles into a publication titled *The Texas Sketchbook*. It was intended only as a Christmas gift for Humble officials and special customers, but it became a collector's item almost immediately.

Although he was an official of an advertising agency, and Humble's magazine was strictly a business venture, Schiwetz refused from the start to categorize himself as either a "documentary" or "commercial" artist. Rather he was a kind of roving collector of Texana, anxious to preserve images of history, but also bringing to life contemporary scenes, and always the Texas countryside that he loved.

Buck had never really liked the business world. He disliked deadlines and he hated the tedium of administration. He liked the money, which now came in sizeable amounts, but he wanted the freedom to find himself as an artist instead of a hired hand. In 1966, he succeeded.

He and Ruby Lee built a hideaway home and studio overlooking the Guadalupe River near Ingram in the Hill Country. There Buck became the free-lance painter he had always wanted to be.

Ruby Lee, a fine artist when they married, now also had an opportunity to develop her own talents. Her sculptures and her paintings won awards in exhibitions and are included in permanent museum collections. She also worked in ceramics,

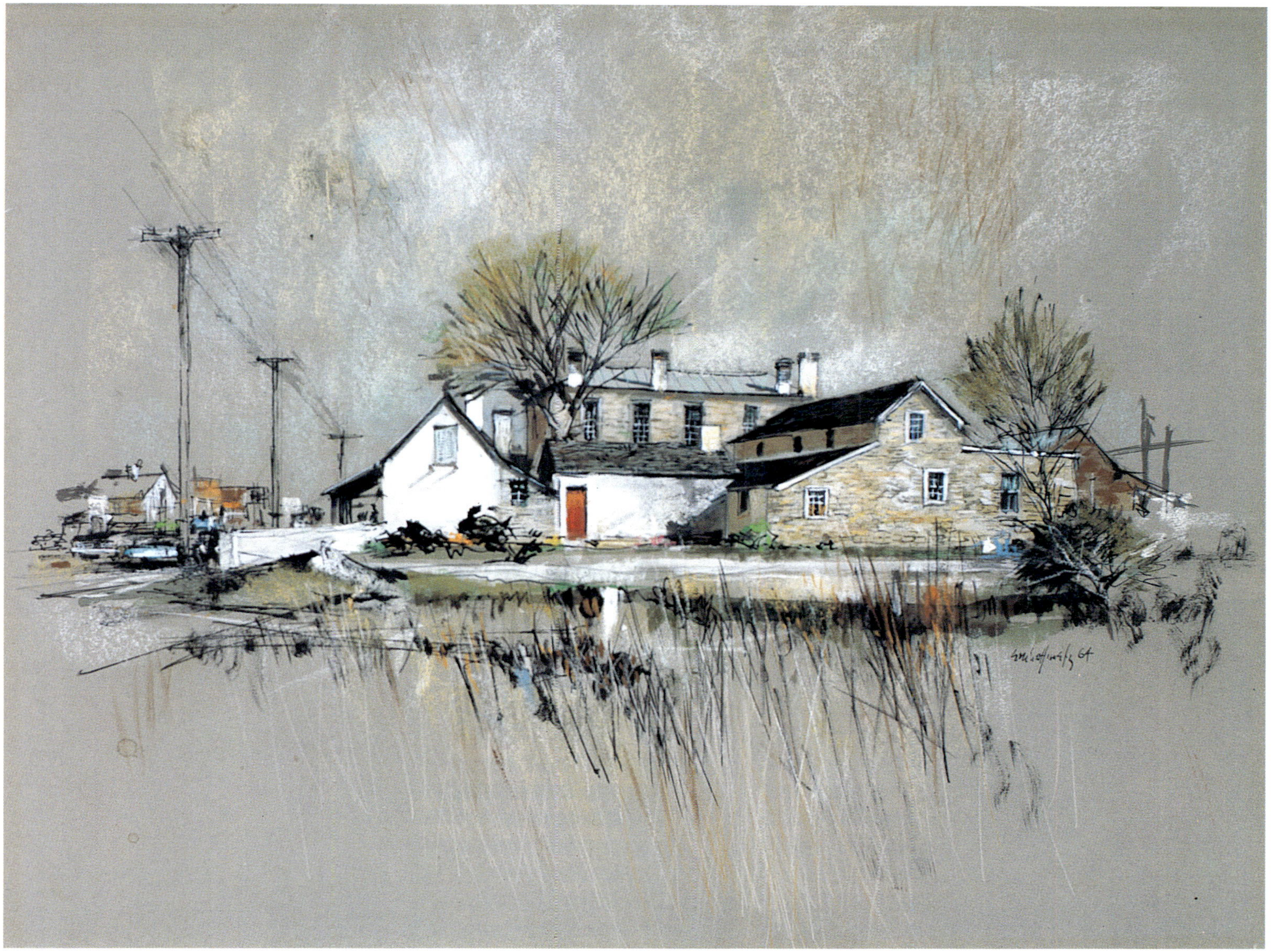

"FREDERICKSBURG PIONEER MUSEUM"
BY BUCK SCHIWETZ
13" X 17" MIXED MEDIA
From the Collection of
Jack and Peggy Moore, Hunt, Texas

mosaics, spinning and weaving and needlepoint, and taught classes in arts and crafts.

The new life also gave Buck a chance to experiment. He had gained national attention for his pencil sketches, an art field often neglected today, and had done some work in other mediums. But now he wanted to explore them all. He used water colors, oil, pencil, his etching tool, acrylics, felt tipped pens, ink washes and even crayons. Whatever he produced sold quickly, usually at four figures.

Schiwetz hated to part with his work. He set his price high and refused to haggle. Once when a prospective buyer wanted him to take less than he was asking, he turned the picture to the wall.

Unfortunately, the so-called "golden years" were hardly that for Buck and Ruby Lee. She developed a mental illness; he became an alcoholic. He recovered thanks to Alcoholics Anonymous. She did not.

He also had a heart attack, followed by a stroke. Then he developed cancer, which left him lame.

He spent his last years at Westhoff (pop. 410) in a one-time gasoline station that he had converted into a two-room home. One room was bedroom, kitchen, library and bathroom combined. The other was a studio filled with an over-sized drawing board and the memorabilia of more than 70 years of putting Texas on paper and canvas.

In his latter years, Schiwetz continued to paint, often as long as eight hours a day. But he was repelled by the thought of selling his works.

"I'm fed up with painting them and never seeing them again," he said. I want to keep them around and enjoy them awhile."

Buck Schiwetz died in his gas station home on August 24, 1984, at the age of 86. He is buried in the State Cemetery in Austin.

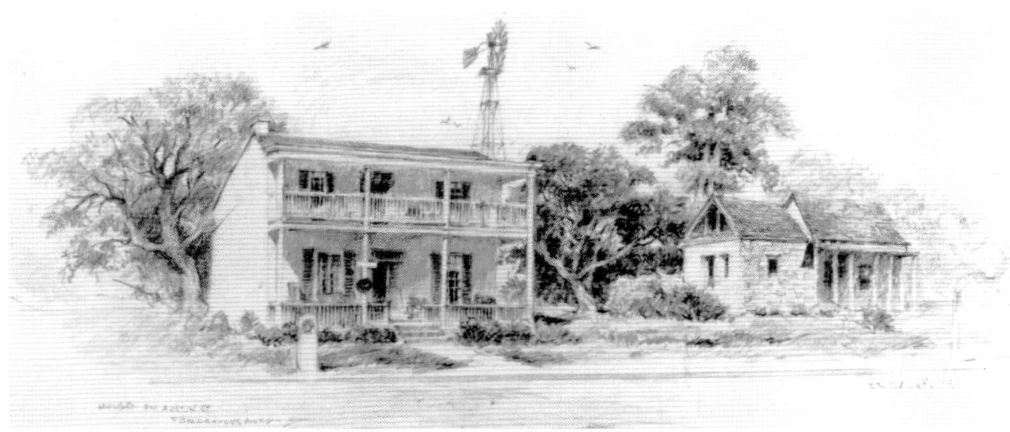

"HOUSE ON AUSTIN STREET,
FREDERICKSBURG, TEXAS 1973"
BY BUCK SCHIWETZ
16 1/2" X 20" CHARCOAL AND PENCIL
From the Collection of
Texas A&M University

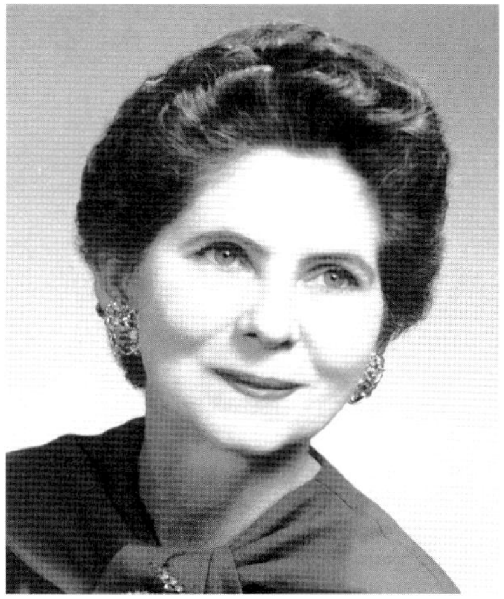

DOLLIE SPIDEL NABINGER
1905-1988

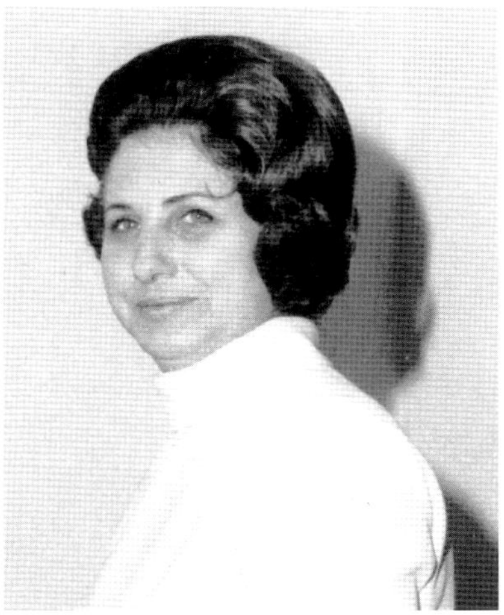

VIRGINIA MULLER
1930-1981
"The Mother-Daughter Artists"

Photos Courtesy of Belton Muller

Most artists say that they owe at least a part of their success to the encouragement of parents. This was true in the case of Dollie Spidel Nabinger and Virginia Nabinger Muller.

Growing up in Victoria where she was born in 1905, Dollie always wanted to be an artist. Her parents encouraged her from childhood, enrolling her in a Catholic school because the public school didn't teach art at the time. Her father personally stretched her first canvases.

Dollie always credited that loving support for her eventual success as an artist. So when her own daughter, Virginia, was born in 1930 and showed an early interest in art, Dollie was her first teacher and her inspiration. They became Fredericksburg's prominent team of mother-daughter artists.

When Dollie was 13, her talent already was so evident that J.F. McCan, a well-known Victoria artist, accepted her as his "apprentice." She studied with him for seven years. Next she was off to the Art Students' League in New York for two years' instruction; later, in San Antonio, she studied with José Arpa, Harry Anthony DeYoung and others. In 1955 she spent a summer in Paris attending classes at the Academie Julian.

Her other teacher was nature itself. She always insisted that studying nature was her greatest learning experience. It inspired her to spend the rest of her life trying to capture on canvas the mountains of Colorado and Wyoming; the pine trees of East Texas; the bluebonnets, the cacti, the live oaks and the rolling hills around Fredericksburg that she loved so well.

In 1942, the Allen Galleries in Houston became her exclusive representative. That relationship continued into the 1950's until George Allen, the owner, died.

Dollie was married to Jack E. Nabinger, a Southern Pacific Railway employee and the grandson of German immigrants. Like many others, Dollie and Jack discovered Fredericksburg almost by chance. Returning from an auto trip to West Texas in 1962, they stopped here for lunch. They had been looking for a place to retire where she could paint and Jack could follow his hobbies of photography and wood-carving. Deciding over lunch that Fredericksburg was the place, they contacted a realtor, bought a house (the Weinheimer home on the corner of Creek and Crockett) and moved here shortly after.

Dollie's paintings continued to sell well. For many years, she painted and conducted workshops from her home, and Jack hand made and carved many of her frames. In 1988, Dollie died, and is buried in the Greenwood Cemetery in Fredericksburg.

Meanwhile the daughter who had been her first student also had become a successful artist.

Born in Skidmore, Texas, (near Beeville) November 6, 1930, Virginia had

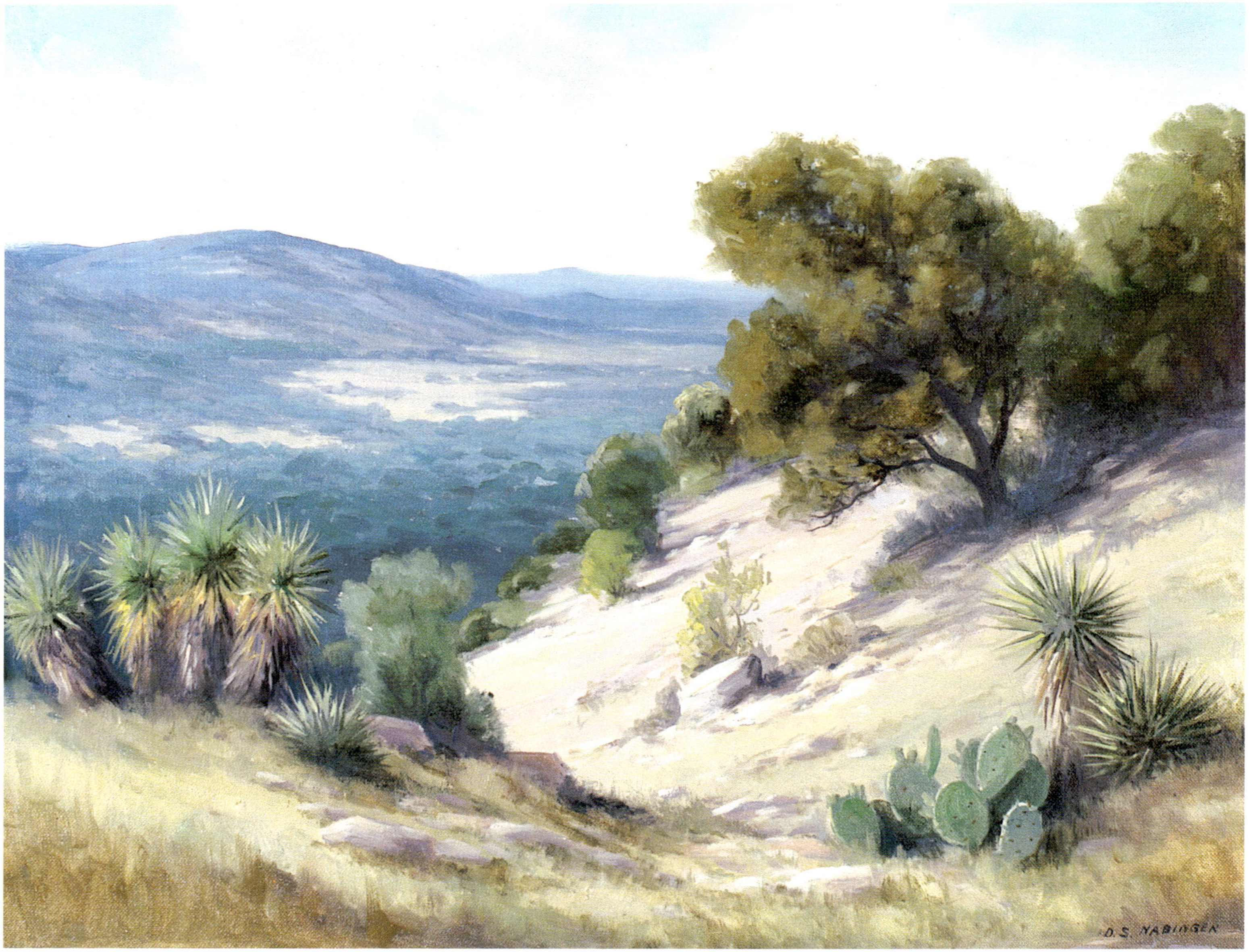

"WILLOW CITY LOOP"
BY DOLLIE SPIDEL NABINGER
16" X 20" OIL ON CANVAS
From the Collection of Belton Muller

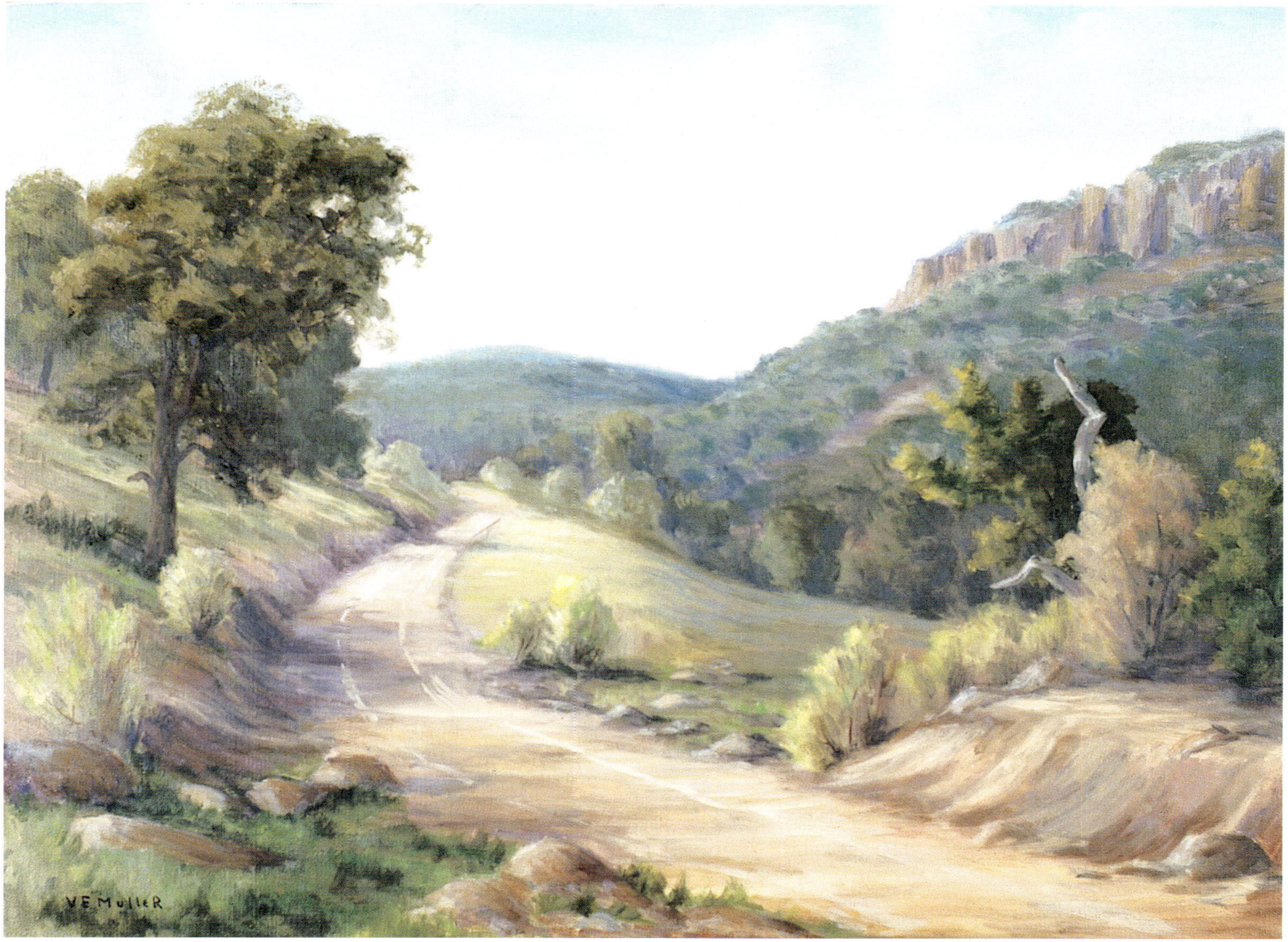

"WILLOW CITY LOOP"
BY VIRGINIA MULLER
18" X 24" OIL ON CANVAS
From the Collection of Sharon Jung

started taking art lessons from her mother at age 10, then studied with Ramon Froman of Dallas, a portrait painter. She graduated from high school in Nacogdoches, Texas, then enrolled at Stephen F. Austin University, where she studied under Janet Turner. She also attended workshops conducted by Frank Reilly, Milford Zornes, Reese Kennedy and George Carpenter, all nationally-known for their work in oil and watercolor.

Virginia married Belton Muller, and they had an art gallery in Kilgore. Belton was associated with a tourists' organization, and he and Virginia traveled extensively with various artists' groups on painting expeditions.

One July, Virginia and Belton drove to Fredericksburg to visit the Nabingers. The temperature was hanging around 100 degrees and the area was in the grip of a drought, making the Mullers wonder why anyone would want to live in climate like the one her parents had chosen.

However, when they returned the next Spring, the weather was moderate and the bluebonnets and other wild flowers were in full bloom. They fell in love with the place and, in 1968, bought a two-story rock house on South Orange, which they remodeled as a residence and gallery. Later a studio was added. They became permanent Fredericksburg residents.

Like her mother, Virginia preferred landscapes and still lifes. Watercolor was her favorite medium. She conducted classes at the Muller Gallery and Studio, and also sponsored watercolor workshops in Saltillo, Mexico.

Virginia and Belton were involved in many Fredericksburg activities, including the Gillespie County Historical Society. For several years they designed and made the decorations and back drops for the annual Masken Ball, for which they were given an award of merit for historical preservation and restoration.

Virginia's works were exhibited by Artist and Craftsman Associated, Dallas; Coppini Academy of Fine Art, San Antonio; Southwestern Watercolor Society, Dallas; Kerrville Art League, and the Hill Country Arts Foundation, Ingram. Many of her paintings were accepted for juried exhibits by the Texas Fine Arts Association and others.

After a lengthy illness, Virginia Muller died in February, 1981. Like her mother, she is buried in Greenwood Cemetery.

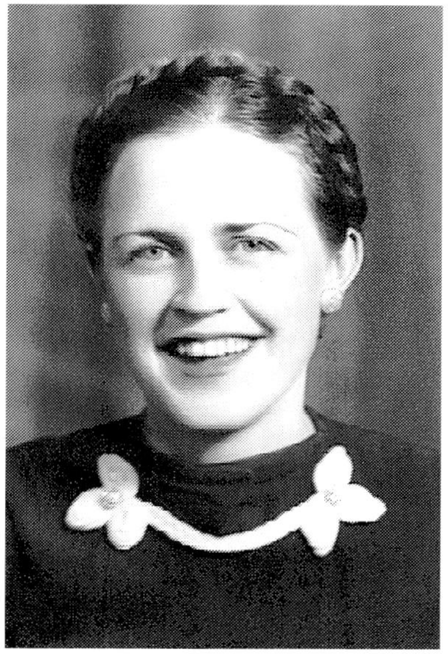

EDNA HELEN BIERSCHWALE
1907-1975
"The Model Artist"

Photo from Private Collection

Edna Helen Bierschwale believed in getting the best possible training for a career in art.

She was born in Comfort, a descendant of four pioneer German families, the daughter of Robert and Martha Flach Bierschwale. She attended public schools there. Classmates, who nicknamed her "Sugar," remember her as a first-rate debater who also played roles in productions of a local drama group.

When very young, Edna had won a local "Prettiest Baby Contest" and her beauty was only enhanced as she grew up. Later she was to become the favorite model of a number of well-known artists.

In 1925, she enrolled in the old Westmoreland College in San Antonio (now a part of Trinity University) but didn't complete the term. In order to get other required courses prior to admission to the Sophie Newcomb College in New Orleans, she enrolled in Fredericksburg High School, and graduated from there in 1926.

Her next stop was Sophie Newcomb College in New Orleans.. She took every art course offered. During the first term she took six classes---pottery, life painting, oil painting, history of painting, design and art composition. The next term she took advanced courses in the history of painting and art composition.

She loved New Orleans, but apparently preferred Texas as a home. Edna returned to Fredericksburg and married Dr. Perry Donop, the physician who built and founded the Fredericksburg Hospital and Clinic. During her Fredericksburg years, she gave private art lessons to a number of local residents in both Fredericksburg and Comfort, and painted numerous scenes in and around the Hill Country.

Her career really took off when she and her husband moved to San Antonio where she continued her studies with José Arpa, Xavier Gonzales, Etienne Ret and Dean Faucett, all well-known local artists.

Edna and her husband were active members of San Antonio's rather large art colony. They owned a beautiful home and entertained often and lavishly. Her parties were described as "wonderful" and were the talk of the city's high society. Her guest book read like a "who's who" of the local art world, and some of the celebrities accompanied their signatures with a humorous sketch.

Her striking beauty inspired many of her talented guests to paint her portrait. She is described as being exceedingly fair in complexion, with a strong face, vibrant green eyes and chestnut hair. Photos of some of these paintings are in the files of The University of Texas Institute of Texan Cultures in San Antonio.

Her paintings were mostly landscapes, florals, and old rock houses. Her chosen medium was water colors, and her style ranged from realistic to the popular impressionistic style of the times. Her painting was of such high quality that she earned an ample income at a time when it was uncommon for women to be self-supporting. She also dabbled in pottery, of which there is only one known surviving piece.

In later years, Edna Bierschwale returned to her beloved Texas Hill Country. She was alone and in ill health. As time passed, her financial resources were depleted, and she was forced to barter her paintings for medical services and other necessities of life.

Today her work is owned and treasured by a number of Comfort residents, and is in the private art collections of many well-known San Antonio art collectors.

Edna died early in 1975 at a nursing home in Fredericksburg, and was simply buried as Edna B. Killion in the Comfort Cemetery.

After her death, Nellie Buell organized a show of Edna's artwork in the Comfort Art

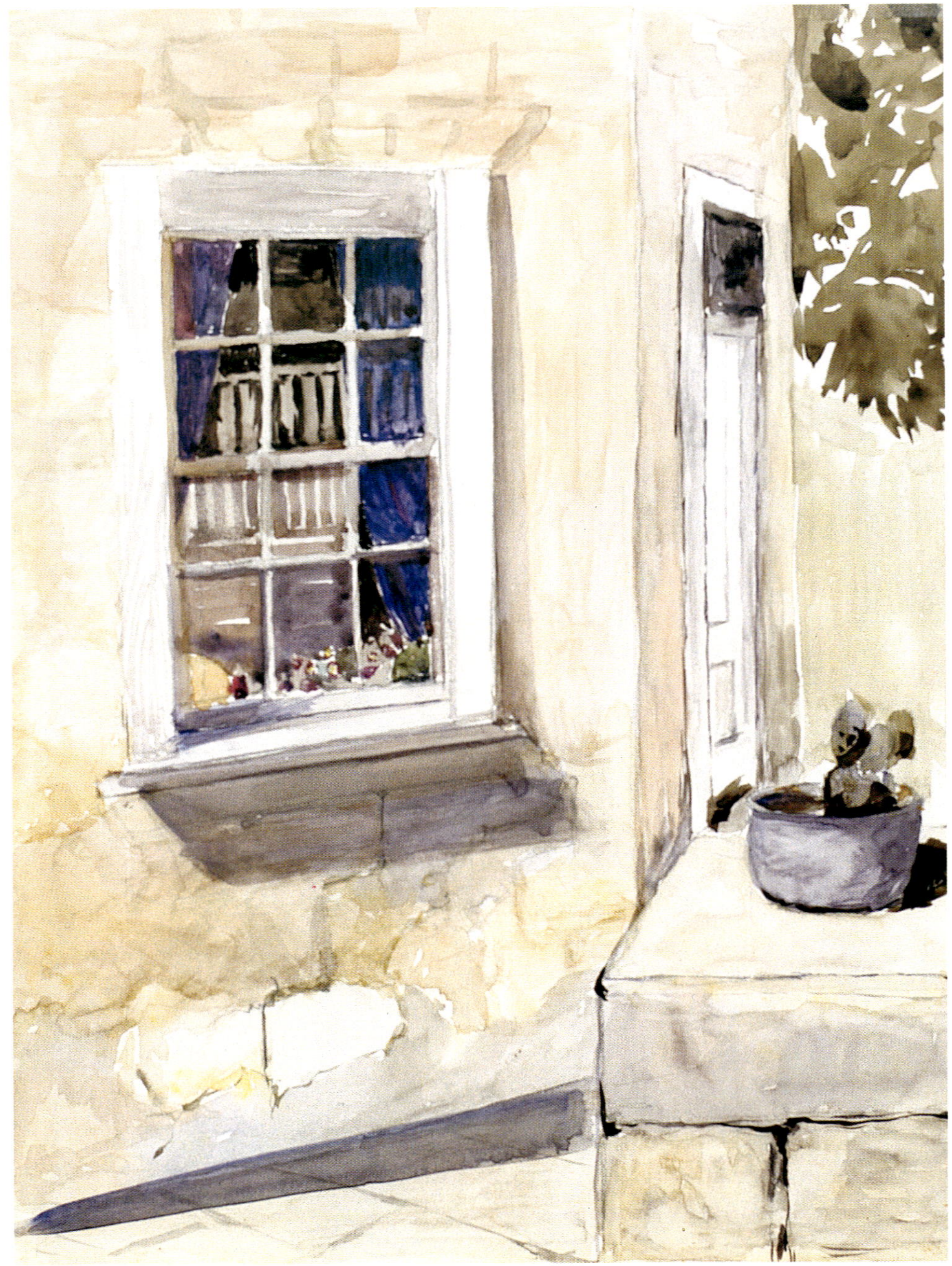

"WINDOW OF OLD ROCK HOUSE"
BY EDNA HELEN BIERSCHWALE
13"x 9 1/2" WATERCOLOR
From Private Collection

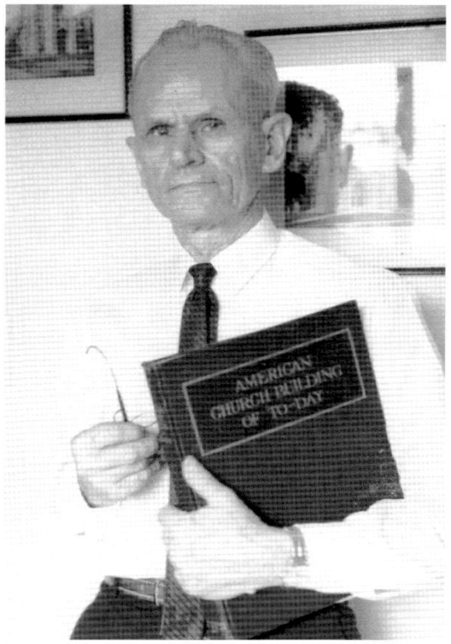

WERNER E. WEBER
1909-1974
"The Cathedral Artist"

Photo Courtesy of
Mrs. Dorothy Ann Weinheimer

Werner Emil Weber was not a painter, but he was an artist. His inborn talent was devoted throughout his life to glorifying God, and to preserving the heritage of Fredericksburg.

From his early childhood, Werner liked to draw and to carve wood. He was also an extremely religious man and felt that he had been called for a special mission in life. This belief was reinforced when, at age nine, he was saved by a premonition from being bitten by a rattlesnake. Gathering bundles of fodder, he suddenly felt an overwhelming sensation warning him that he should not touch the bundle that he was starting to pick up. When his father investigated, they found a huge rattlesnake, poised to strike, hidden there. To Werner, the rattler represented "certain death," from which God spared him for a purpose.

As a young man, Werner became a wood worker in Stein's Lumber Mill in Fredericksburg. He became fascinated with art and architecture, and was one of the first historical preservationists in Fredericksburg. During the 1920's and 1930's, he managed to photograph virtually all of the pioneer homes and buildings still standing in and around the town. From his photos, he made pencil sketches---sketches which were used as reference by John McClusky when he painted the town's historical buildings as part of the celebration of the 125th Anniversary of Fredericksburg's founding.

Long before historical preservation was a popular cause, Werner believed that the heritage of his home and people should be cherished. For most of his life he was a lone voice urging the Chamber of Commerce to prevent the demolition of older homes and buildings.

Werner's love of beauty and design also permeated his religious life. Even as a teenager attending Fredericksburg's Zion Lutheran Church, he was disturbed by the drab colors and design of the furnishings. This made him "long for an opportunity to someday make the interior nice." Although he had never been in other churches, he somehow felt that they must be beautiful, and he wanted his church to look the same.

For years he made drawings of how he thought the interior and the reredos might be improved. When he was satisfied with the design, he prayed that God would move the heart of someone who would give the money needed to make the changes. Years went by and nothing happened.

"(But) God works in mysterious ways," he would recall later. In 1962, the congregation decided to remodel the church. Werner not only was asked to serve on the committee for the project, but he did all the woodwork in the sanctuary. He built the pulpit, baptismal, communion railing and kneeler, and designed and built the altar.

That was only the beginning. He made many lecterns and chancel furnishings

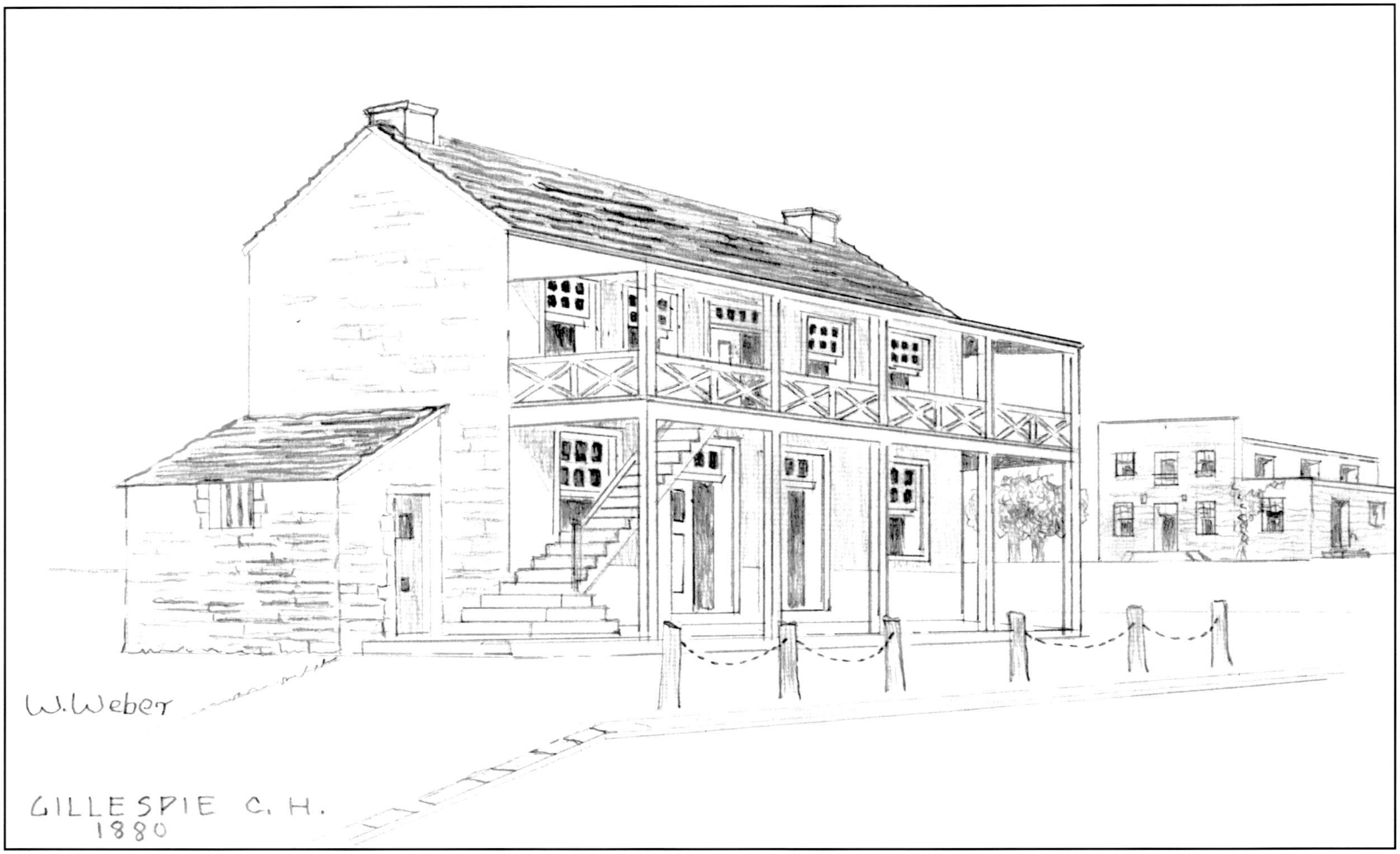

"GILLESPIE COURT HOUSE 1880"
BY WERNER E. WEBER
6 3/4" X 10" PENCIL DRAWING
Courtesy of
Mrs. Dorothy Ann Weinheimer

for other local churches---all donated by him. As gifts to the parish, he designed and hand carved both the outside and inside symbols for Fredericksburg's St. Barnabas Episcopal Church.

Because of his love for beautiful churches, Weber began collecting picture post cards of them. Over 20 years, he collected more than 25,000 views of more than 10,000 different places of worship. He cataloged the collection and gave it to the Smithsonian Institution in 1972.

As a youngster growing up in a small German settlement in rural Texas, Werner often wondered why the United States didn't have cathedrals like those that are so common in Europe. Then he discovered in 1920 that the National Cathedral was being built in Washington, D.C. and that it would be one of the world's largest. As soon as he could, he went to see it.

He would return on several occasions, once spending four consecutive days exploring it. Entranced with the beautiful building, he wanted to make a contribution for its support. Money was out of the question. His only income came from his employment in the shop of the Stein Lumber Company. So he offered to hand carve a lectern as his gift.

The lectern not only was accepted, but it pleased the Dean of the cathedral so much that he requested Werner do a second one to be used in the Bethlehem Chapel. He was honored to comply. Made of light oak with a satin finish, it bore the inscription, "For Your Great Glory, May This Work of My Hands Please You."

In addition to the lecterns, Weber donated his entire collection of ecclesiastical books on cathedral architecture and art, some 200 volumes, to the Washington Cathedral.

"I was able to apply the talent God placed in me," he said. "I hope He is pleased with the work of my hands."

"The great love to make His house attractive...is a thing placed in me by God," he said once. "God calls men into the ministry to preach His Word, so I feel that God has called me to make his house attractive."

Weber died in 1974 and is buried in Fredericksburg.

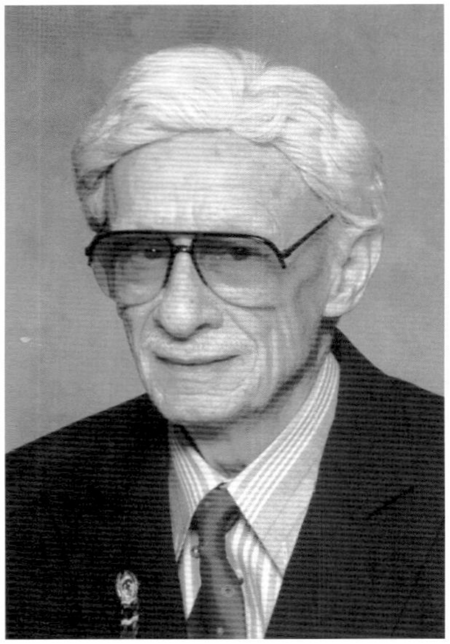

GOTTHOLD G. LENTZ
1912-
"Historic Artist"

Photo Courtesy of Gotthold Lentz

His father's calling as a minister of the Gospel brought Gotthold G.H. Lentz to Fredericksburg from his native Nebraska. He remained to record much of the community's early history on canvas and paper.

Born March 19, 1912, in Nebraska, he was 17 when his father, due to illness, had to retire as a Lutheran minister in Fredericksburg. In 1942, Lentz joined the U.S. Army and served four years during World War II. He returned here after the war.

He had been interested in painting since childhood, and decided, after the war ended, to follow art as a profession. He studied at the San Antonio Art Institute, and painted in water color, oil and acrylic.

Lentz began painting Fredericksburg scenes early on. Some of his earliest work was done from two photographs taken around the turn of the century showing local street scenes. The photos were taken by F.J. Maier, who had a mercantile store on the present site of the Keidel Memorial Clinic. The pictures were black and white and had no people in them.

One is a view down West Main with the *Vereins Kirche* in the distance. The other looks east toward the Nimitz Hotel. In Lentz's paintings, he brought the street alive with people and activities. Both of these brilliant water colors were made into picture post cards to celebrate Fredericksburg's 125th anniversary in 1971.

In 1952, Lentz moved to Sinton where he built a studio and taught art in the local schools. He taught art at Bellville and Brenham for several years.

During these years, Lentz completed many paintings of historical interest for business firms and private collectors. The South Central Savings of Brenham commissioned him to do a number of large paintings depicting the history of that area. One of his religious murals hangs in the Lutheran Seminary in Fremont, Nebraska.

Lentz has had many one-man art shows. One year he was selected as "Artist of the Month" by the Corpus Christi Fine Arts Colony. He has been asked to judge at many art shows and served several times as chair of local Art and Craft Shows.

Although his teaching took him to other areas of Texas, Lentz was never very far from Fredericksburg in memory. He made paintings of many local homes for their owners. His rendition of Fort Martin Scott as it may have looked during the Civil War hangs in the *Vereins Kirche* Museum here.

When the *Lincoln-Mercury Times* published an article on Fredericksburg Sunday houses several years ago, the magazine chose two of Lentz's paintings to illustrate the story. A companion magazine, *Ford Times*, also used Lentz's paintings of restaurants in San Antonio and Corpus Christi.

In the 1950's, his painting of the *Vereins Kirche* as it may have appeared on a snowy night in the early years, became a Christmas card produced by the Fredericksburg Publishing Co. It is still a popular seller today.

Stonewall and Luckenbach have also been subjects for his work. Lentz never married. Today he shares a Stonewall home with his sister, Maggie.

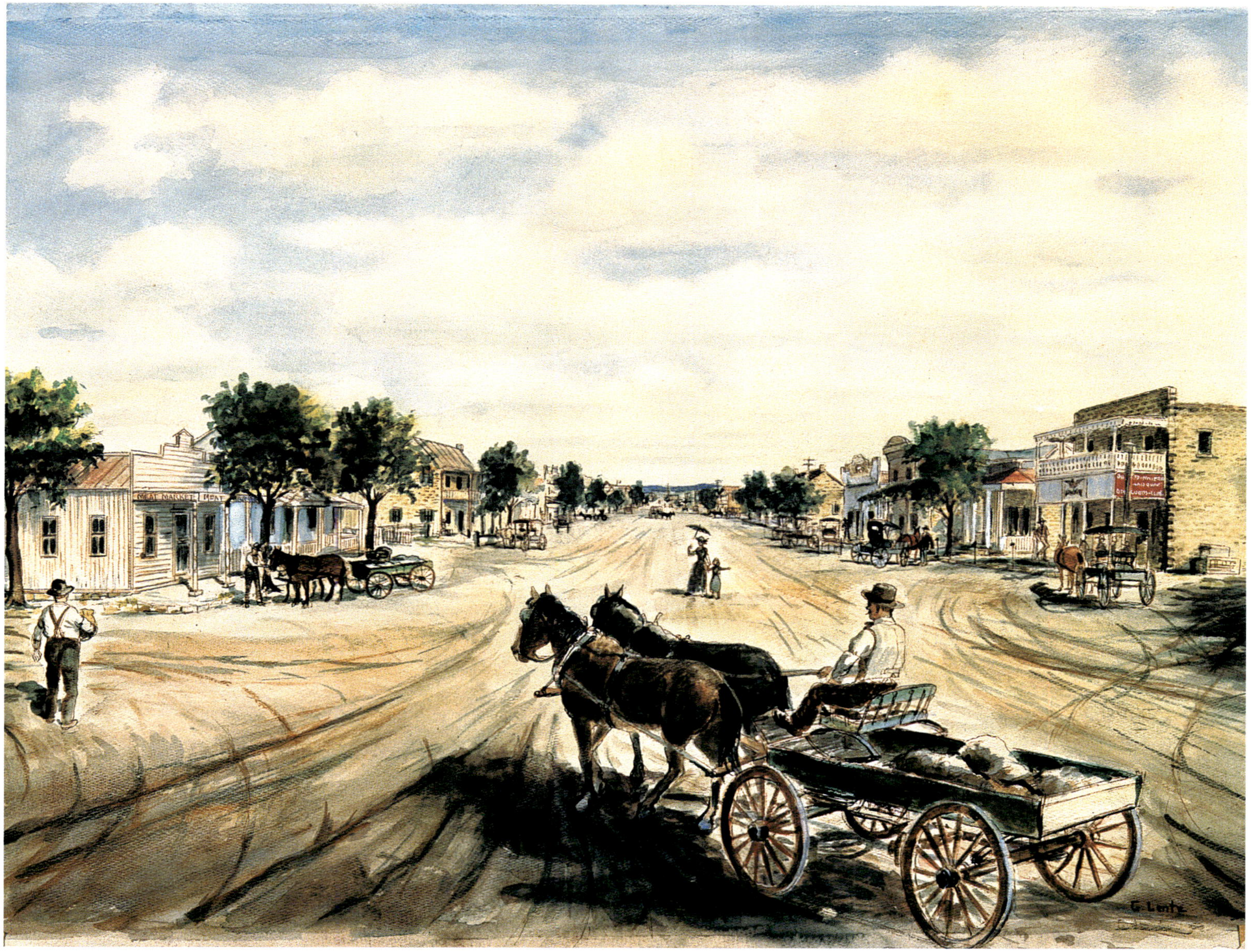

"MAIN STREET"
BY GOTTHOLD LENTZ
22" X 27" WATERCOLOR
From the Collection of the
Udo Henke Family

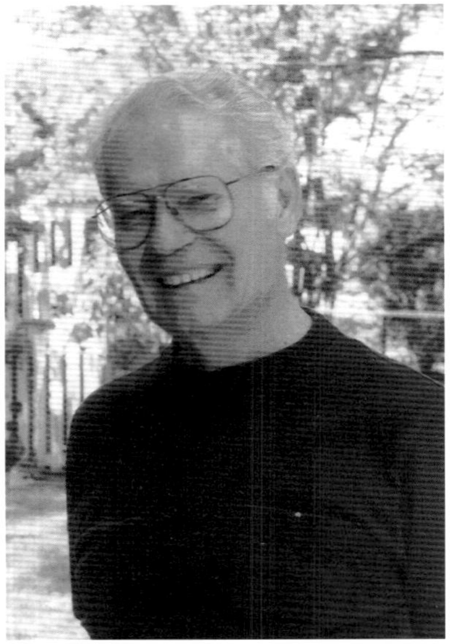

JOHN D. McCLUSKY
1914-1994
"The Spiritual Artist"

Photo Courtesy of Mrs. John McClusky

John D. McClusky was a Connecticut Yankee who discovered Fredericksburg in 1970, liked it and stayed on to devote the rest of his professional life to documenting the culture and heritage of the town and its people. And he would do it in a unique way.

To begin with, he was a deeply religious man (he was, in fact, an ordained minister). To him, all of life was a celebration of God's love for his creation and humanity. McClusky saw his art as a divine calling---a vehicle for the appropriate expression of that love.

Yet he didn't dedicate his tremendous talent to painting churches, icons or religious talismans. Instead he sought to explore the creative spirit by painting people and things. He was fascinated by the character and personalities of ordinary people, and they served as the inspiration and sometimes the subject of his work.

As one writer, David Syring, said of him:

"His paintings, more than being pictures of things seen through the eyes, are tracings of one human being's experience of a world full of light, of damage and healing, of possibility and of love. It is only in this context---in the world of richly felt, deeply thought and fully embraced experience---that John's life and his work as a painter can be understood."

McClusky was part painter and part philosopher. Born September 28, 1914, in East Haven, Connecticut, his Catholic parents were of stern German background and modest means, and wanted their son to grow up a success.

As a child, John knew he wanted to be an artist. He filled the walls in his room with drawings. When no paper was available, he drew figures and buildings on the window shades, much to the chagrin of his parents. By the time he had finished high school, he knew that he had to become an artist.

From 1933 to 1936, he was enrolled at Ohlm's School of Fine Arts in New Haven. The school was affiliated with Yale University and was experimental. McClusky recalled that classes went on from 8 A.M. to 11 P.M. seven days a week. Students did everything from designing commercial displays to painting in the classical style. In three years, the only holidays were Easter and Christmas Day. He remembered it as being equal to six years in a college.

When he left Ohlm's school, he enrolled in Colgate University for two years and then did commercial art with a friend. They designed packages and other material for several national accounts. By 1961, however, John had to come to a decision:

"Either I had to drop dead or spend the rest of my life painting," he recalled. He took the latter route.

After using oils, egg tempera, casein, pastels, watercolors and mixed media, John settled on acrylic polymer. He felt it was ideal because it dries (almost)

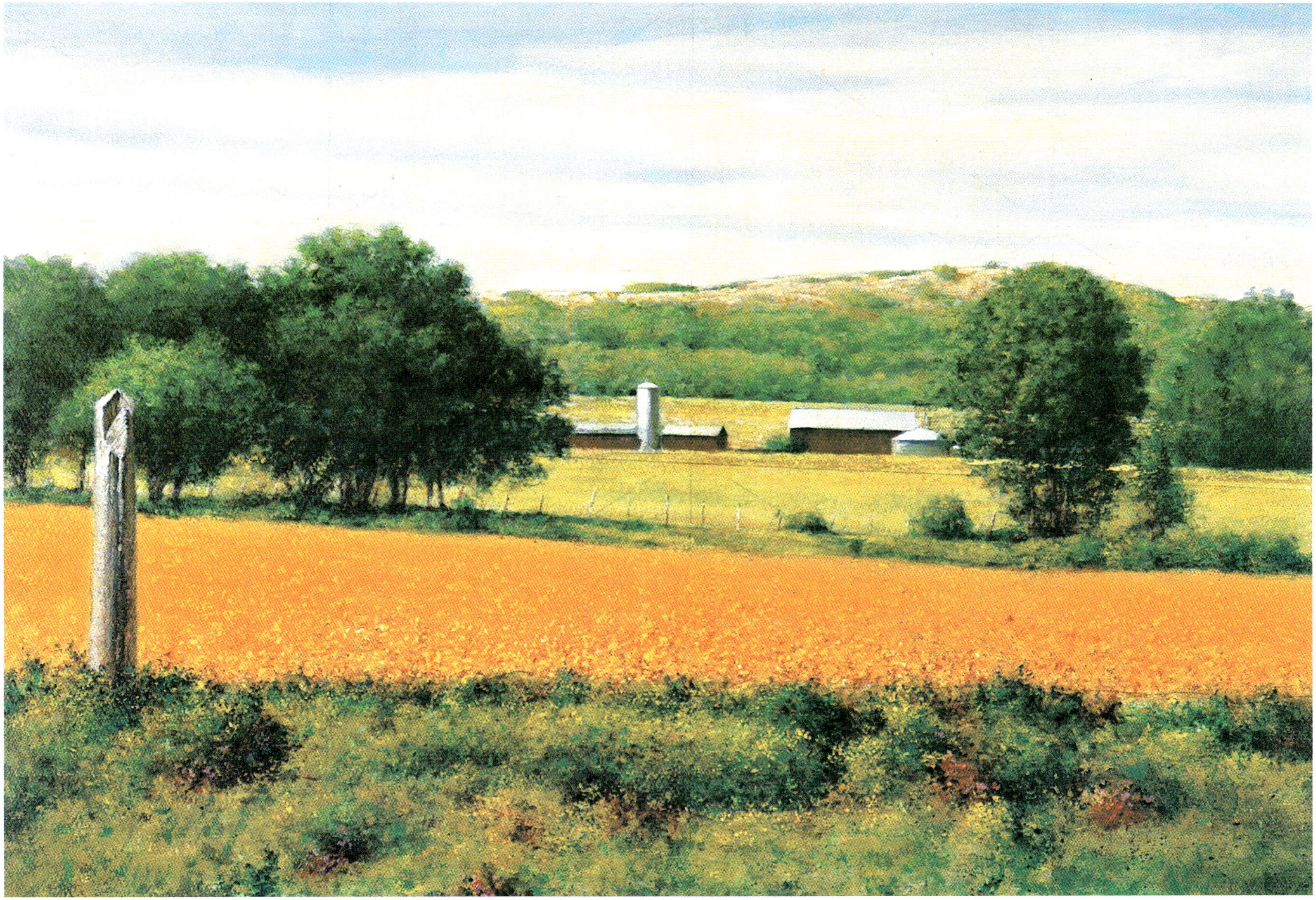

"COSMOS" (UNFINISHED)
BY JOHN McCLUSKY
18" X 27 1/4"
ACRYLIC ON WATERCOLOR PAPER
From the Collection of Mrs. John McClusky

immediately; the chemical reactions of the colors cease when the paint dries, whereas oil paints continue to react for years; the artist can apply many glazes, one right after the other, as the paint dries; and paintings can be cleaned with mild soap and water, keeping the colors clear for decades.

He knew, too, that he would be a realist both in his technique and in offering his work to the public. He always preferred to sell his works to museums or collections rather than to individuals.

"A painting becomes a dead painting in the possession of one person only," was his philosophy. He did, however, sell to private collectors such as the late actor, Henry Fonda; the Forbes Magazine collection, and a few others.

Although his paintings of both New England and Texas scenes reflect his dedication to realism, his philosophy also comes through to those sensitive to fine art. When he was very young, McClusky discovered the writings of Thoreau and Emerson and they left a lasting impression. They generated in him a quest for greater understanding of the times in which we live and the uncertain position of man in relation to the universe.

That's why he always insisted that one must go beyond the visual level of art in order to appreciate it properly.

In 1970, McClusky, 56 years old and already a success in New England, decided to find a new base. He and his wife, Lois, drove 4,500 miles around the country before discovering Fredericksburg. For them and the two children still at home, it was the Nirvana they were seeking.

It was, in his words, "an old German community which still has many of the characteristics that identified it more than a century ago. It's...the kind of life that you don't see too often today."

Once settled in, McClusky began painting the people and the town. He started exploring the creative spirit---a potential he said he saw manifested in each person's service to one's family, one's community and one's God.

He walked Fredericksburg streets looking for simple, yet important subjects to paint. He wanted to bring them to the attention of the people to help them better understand their heritage and to appreciate it more.

In 1971, when Fredericksburg observed the 125th anniversary of its founding, McClusky had each member of his art class paint an historic building. The landmarks were a feature attraction of the celebration. (He offered free art classes to talented students for more than 20 years).

On one of his walks, he discovered a child's grave in the Catholic Cemetery. The tiny grave was a simple one, but in front of the headstone was a diminutive figure of a child. That the figure had lasted so many years touched McClusky (who had now become a Lutheran). He painted the figure, saying it "symbolized the kind of love that reaches out beyond the grave."

He described this kind of work as a "community" painting, of which he did many.

Another of his "community" paintings was of a window in an old Sunday house a couple of blocks off Main Street. To McClusky, it was a paradox. As the old house, once used by farmers who came to town for shopping and church on weekends, was coming closer and closer to destruction, the window had become more beautiful as time and vines took over the decaying structure.

The artist called it "Queen's Crown." The townspeople of Fredericksburg were so taken with it that funds were raised by popular subscription to purchase the work. It now hangs in the public library.

This gesture by his neighbors pleased him. He always said that his only goal was to communicate with the people, but admitted that it wasn't easy to do.

"I can't paint without someone making it intelligible," he said. "Otherwise all they see is a pretty picture, and I'm not interested in a pretty picture."

When the community bought "Queen's Crown" to keep it as a part of Fredericksburg forever, McClusky knew that his message was coming through.

McClusky was a successful artist. His paintings today hang in many museums and private collections. Although he made a living from his art, making money was not his primary goal.

"The power to change the human heart is far greater than making money," he said.

Judged by this standard, John McClusky was an unqualified success.

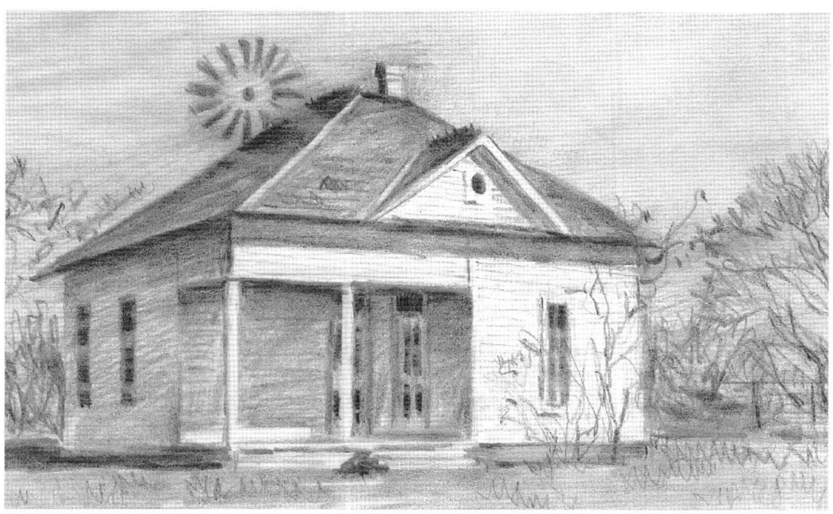

PENCIL SKETCH
BY JOHN McCLUSKY
Courtesy of Mrs. John McClusky

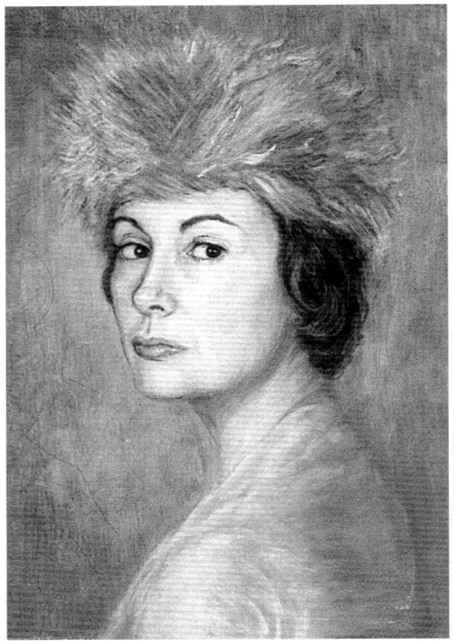

ELSA MURANYI INGELS
1916-
"Like Father, Like Daughter"

ELSA MURANYI INGELS - SELF PORTRAIT
VAN EYCKS TECHNIQUE 1963
Courtesy of Elsa Muranyi Ingels

Elsa Muranyi Ingels is not an artist by chance. She was the only student that Count Gustav Muranyi de Temes, the famed portraitist from Austria-Hungary, ever had.

Muranyi was the artist who painted England's nobility and America's high society during the era of the Vanderbilts. He was as well known in New York and Palm Beach as he was in London. The rich, famous and noted vied to have him do their portraits. He painted the only portrait ever made of Marconi, the Italian inventor of the wireless telegraph.

He also happened to be the father, as well as the first teacher, of Elsa Muranyi Ingels of Fredericksburg, now a renowned artist in her own right.

Elsa Ingels was a long time finding her way to a permanent home in the Texas Hill Country. She was born September 22, 1916 in New York after her parents (her mother was from Wales) had moved to the United States from London. She attended the Gardner School for Girls, the Grand Central School of Art, Florida Southern College and the University of Missouri.

Her life as a student changed one night at a party. When she entered a room full of guests, a handsome young man turned to a friend and boasted:

"I'm going to marry that girl!"

His name was Frank Ingels, a young electronics engineer, and he made good on the boast. The two were married and began a partnership that took them to many parts of the world and lasted until Frank's death in 1981.

They worked together as commentators on a Jacksonville, Florida, radio station. During World War II, while Frank worked for the Sperry Gyroscope Co. on Long Island, New York, Elsa was a draftsman for the same company in radar research. Later Frank joined RCA and the pair left for Europe where he was assigned to the company's international division. When the U.S. State Department needed expert help, RCA loaned Frank to the government.

He was sent to Greece with the Joint U.S. Military Aid Group to help establish communications services for that country's Air Force. During their four years there, Elsa taught in the Anglo-American School. Her students were children of U.S. military, embassy staff and employees of oil companies.

When Frank's Greek assignment ended, the couple moved to Wiesbaden, Germany, where he was in Intelligence. Elsa took advantage of the opportunity and studied with Herr Herzfield. He taught her the 500-year-old technique of the Van Eycks and of the old German masters, who used egg emulsion and oil glazes.

From Germany, the Ingels went to Cape Canaveral, Florida, where he was assigned to the Space Center until his retirement. Then the couple traveled the States, Canada and Mexico for two years before settling in the Taos, New Mexico, art colony in 1967. There, Elsa painted portraits of Indians for Jane Hiatt's widely

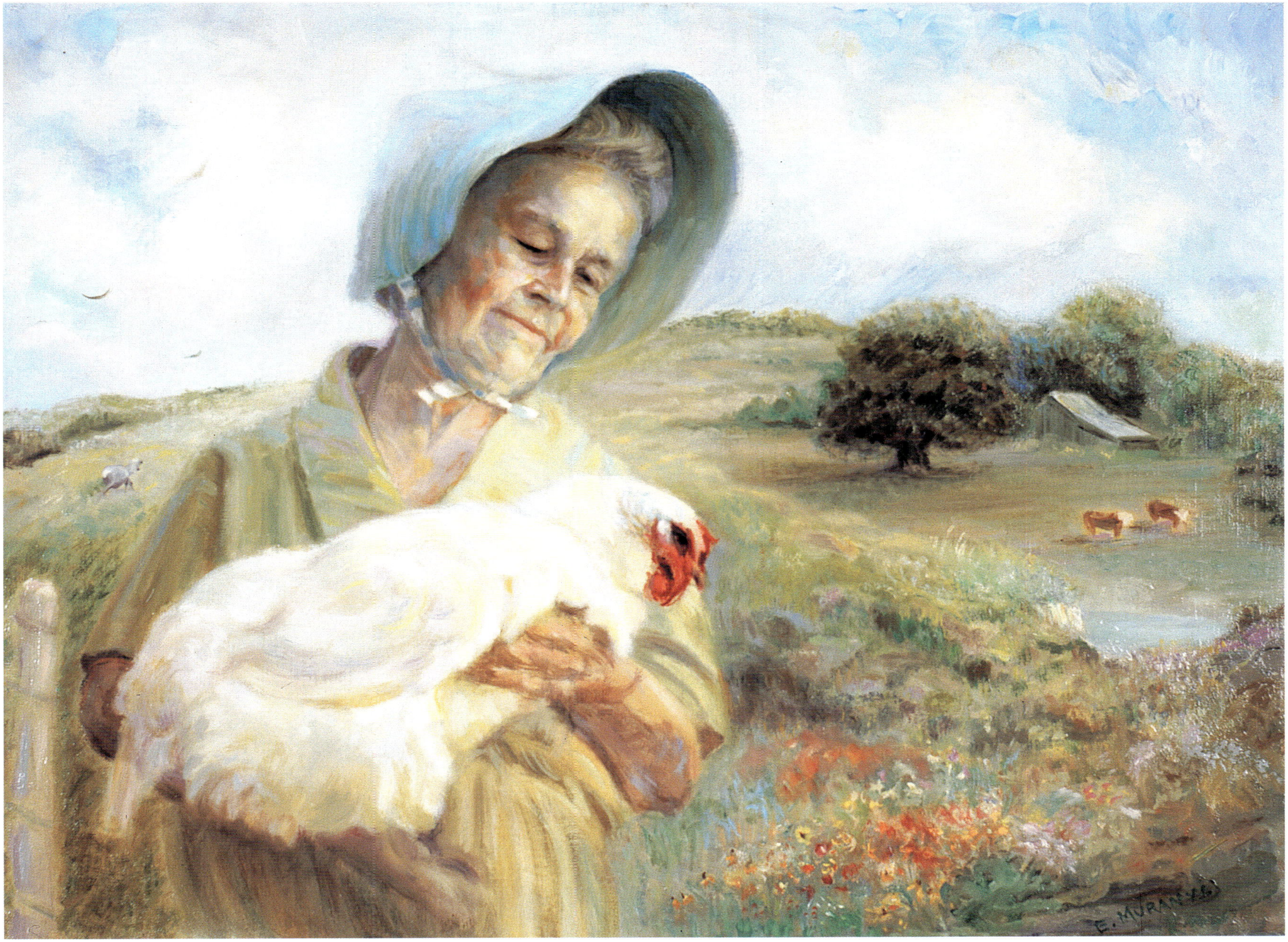

"HER WEALTH"
BY ELSA MURANYI INGELS
18" X 24" VAN EYCKS TECHNIQUE
From the Collection of
Elsa Muranyi Ingels

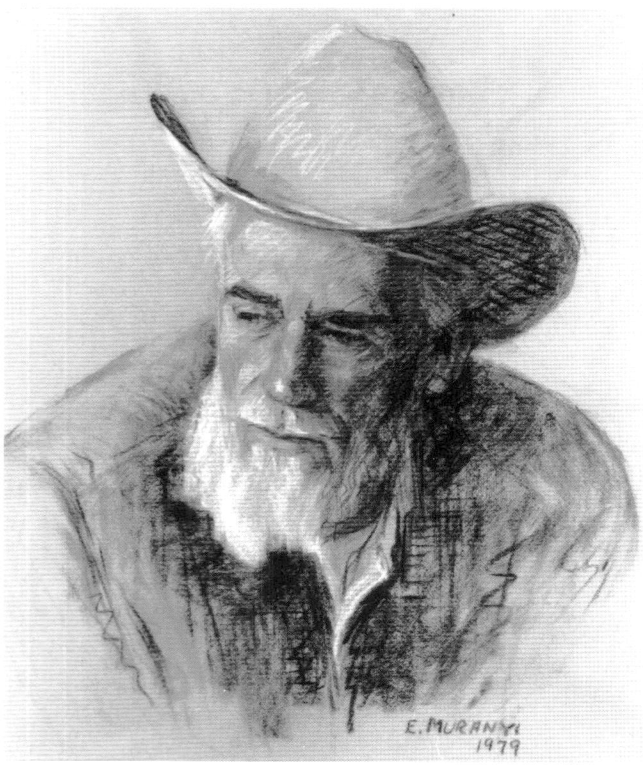

"BELOVED"(FRANK INGELS)
BY ELSA MURANYI INGELS
CHARCOAL ON PAPER
From the Collection of
Elsa Muranyi Ingels

known Village Gallery. She also exhibited in the R.C. Gorman Gallery.

In 1971, they did another tour of Europe and settled temporarily in Geneva, Switzerland, where she studied at the *Ecole de Beaux Arts*. Returning to the States after a year, they spent some time at a Navajo Indian reservation in Arizona so Elsa could paint. There, a teacher with the Bureau of Indian Affairs who was from Luling, Texas, suggested that they look at the Texas Hill Country as a possible retirement spot.

They took the advice, came, saw and were conquered by Fredericksburg. It became their permanent home in 1972.

In an interview after they moved to Fredericksburg, the Ingels told a reporter that their experience living among the Indians introduced them to a way of life that transcends the topsy-turvy world all around us. The artist and her husband said that they found here the same harmony among people, and between people and nature, that exists on the reservations. They found this to be one of the aspects that makes Fredericksburg such a fine place to live.

The paintings Elsa has done since moving to Fredericksburg are reminiscent of the work of her first teacher, her famous father. Signing her work with her maiden name, Elsa Muranyi, she paints primarily in oils, but like her father, has done portraits and sketches in charcoal and pastels. His portraits were character studies and so are many of hers. She has his same ability to bring out the inner being that hides behind the faces of her subjects.

One of her favorite and best-known paintings is that of Rettie Mauldin holding a chicken. Mrs. Mauldin, a Hill Country pioneer, loved her chickens.

"One day I saw the love on her face as she held one of her chickens," Elsa recalls. "I had to paint it!"

She called it "Her Wealth" and it is one of her most beautiful and sensitive character studies. Rettie's love for the bird shines through.

Elsa Muranyi portraits, landscapes and sketches hang in homes throughout Texas and a number of other states. As a member of the Coppini Academy of Fine Arts in San Antonio, her paintings have been recognized twice with first and second place awards. She has been exhibited in many galleries.

Mrs. Ingels continues to paint, expressing the atmosphere of the Hill Country and of Fredericksburg, which has been her home for the longest period of her active life.

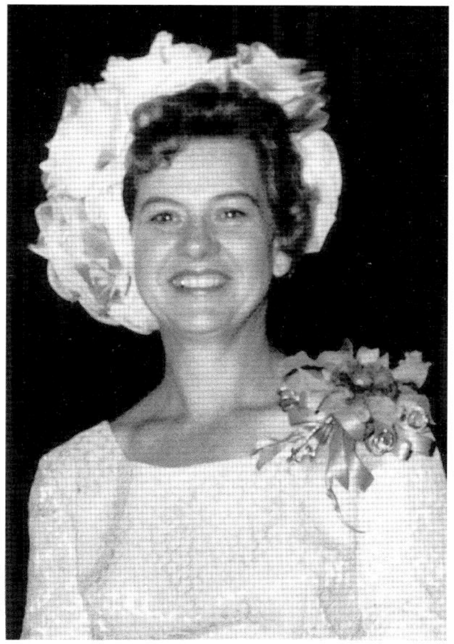

ONIETA MERRIE BARTHOLMAE
1918-1982
"The Housewife Artist"

Photo Courtesy of
Mary Lou Bartholmae Philippus

Onieta Bartholmae was an artist who never took a lesson.

Growing up in the Rio Grande Valley, she was surrounded by flowers. Her mother fancied roses especially, and it was the rose that Onieta loved best of all to paint. When she was only six, she would rush home from school in San Benito, select a rose from the family garden and draw it in great detail.

When she was 17, it was her painting of a single rose that changed her life work from being a successful beautician to an even more successful artist.

That was the year she moved to Fredericksburg with her mother and step-father Dr. James Dickie, an osteopath. Born in Fergus Falls, Minnesota, Onieta had moved to Texas with her parents when she was only four. Now she was making the third move of her young life to an area far different from the lush valley of the Rio Grande. In Fredericksburg, the family lived two houses down from the old jail house on San Antonio Street.

She looked forward to a career as a beautician and customers were quick to come. One liked the personality of the pretty, sandy-haired blonde so much that she invited her to her church---the First Baptist. There she introduced Onieta to her son, Varnell Bartholmae, and romance flourished. They were married. Varnell operated a grocery store on East Main.

It was about the same time that Onieta painted that single red rose. Her "canvas" was a piece of brown wrapping paper, but it seemed to be a perfect background for the flower. She began giving more time to art, developing her natural talent and taking some field trips with established artists.

Onieta painted in oils, water colors and tempera and she especially liked to do still life renditions of flowers, and landscapes with lots of flora. She discovered, however, that she liked to paint anything, including walls. Her paintings soon covered the walls of the bathrooms of her home, Varnell's grocery store and even the First Baptist Church.

At the church she painted Noah's Ark on a wall of the children's Sunday school class. On adjoining walls, she painted the animals heading toward the ark. In another room, she painted a view of the church alongside a Bible and some favorite hymns.

Onieta and Varnell had four children, two boys and two girls. Her artistic talent was manifest even in the clothes she sewed for her family, beautiful creations usually made from her own designs and put together without a pattern. Field trips into the countryside were often turned into family outings, with Onieta's mother knitting and the children playing or taking photographs while Onieta painted the old rock homes or landscapes of her beloved hill country.

A favorite story recalls that one Christmas, when the children were small, Onieta decided to make a life-size Nativity scene for their front yard. She molded the

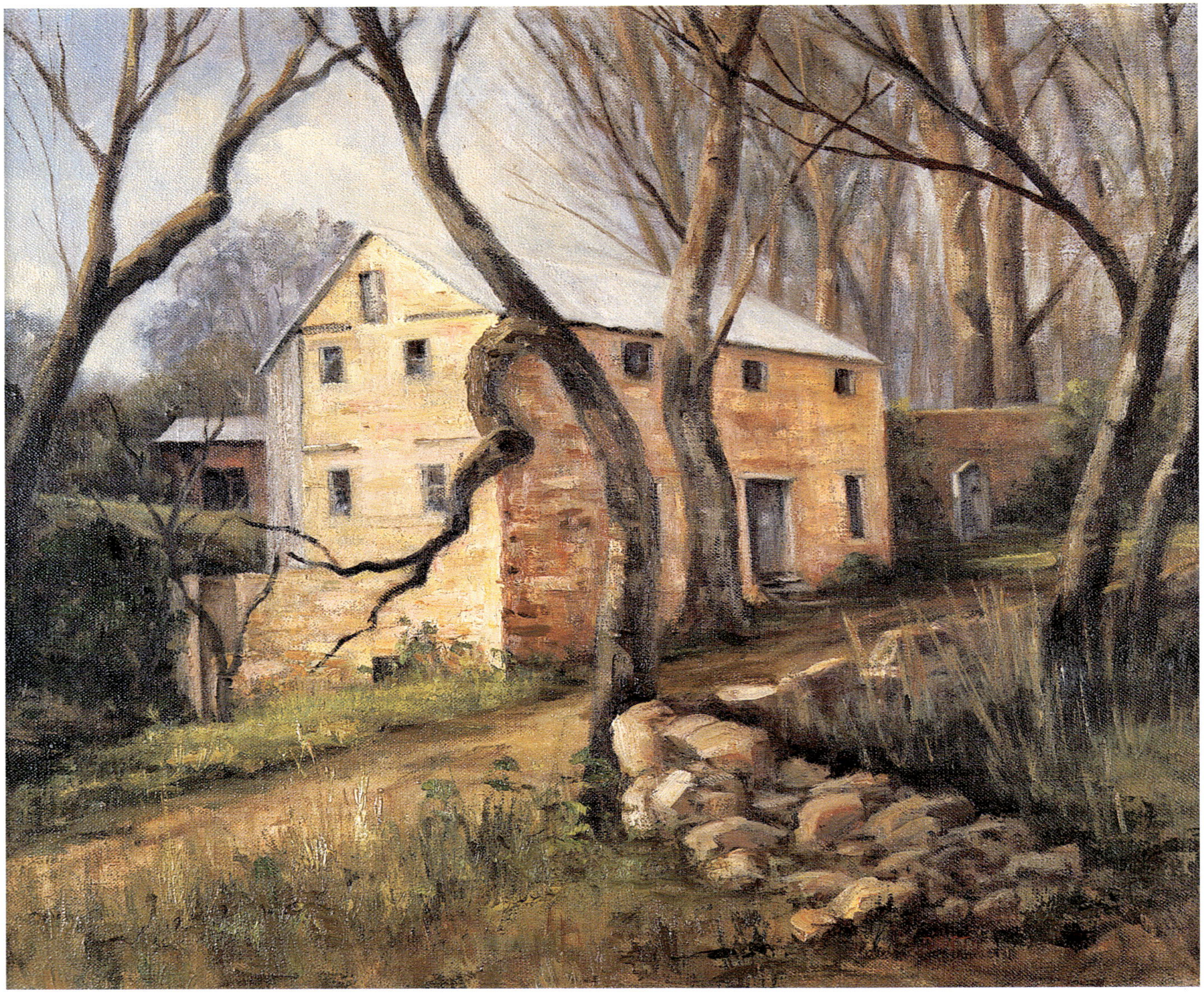

"LANGE'S MILL"
BY ONIETA BARTHOLMAE
21" X 25 1/4" OIL ON CANVAS
From the Collection of
Dr. and Mrs. David Hardison

heads of Mary, Joseph, Baby Jesus and the three wise men from clay, and painted them in exquisite detail. the final step was to dry the clay by baking in the oven.

Varnell's brother, Al, usually came to their home for lunch. On the day of the baking, Onieta was not in the kitchen when Al arrived, and, smelling something cooking, he opened the oven door to see what was for lunch. Imagine his surprise to see six life-size heads roasting in the oven!

The unique churches of Fredericksburg had special appeal to her talents since she gave God credit for her artistic gift. Onieta drew pen and ink pictures of several churches and other landmarks, then donated the drawings to the Hill Country Hospital Auxiliary to be converted into note cards and sold as fund-raisers.

Meanwhile her paintings were attracting public attention. Galleries in Fredericksburg, Austin, Salado and San Antonio began handling her work. Clients came from as far away as California to purchase her landscapes.

She became interested in china painting and taught classes in this medium. She was invited to participate in a number of shows in Austin, San Antonio and elsewhere. Onieta Bartholmae, the beautician, had become Onieta Bartholmae, the artist. She was invited to membership in the Texas Fine Arts Association, the Hill Country Arts Foundation, the Kerrville Art Club and the River Art Group in San Antonio. At an art show in Gonzales, one of the judges made the notation that Onieta Bartholmae was the "only artist that could capture the true color of the cactus on canvas."

An unexpected honor came after her death in June, 1982. Her husband received a letter from *La Louvre* in Paris. They were planning a show of United States artists and asked that one of her paintings be sent for consideration. Varnell didn't want to part with her work even for a short period. He failed to respond.

In 1983, the request from the world famous museum was repeated. Again Varnell declined to respond. No further invitations came from the *Louvre*.

If her work had been submitted and accepted, Onieta Bartholmae would have been the first and only Fredericksburg artist to have been recognized in this way.

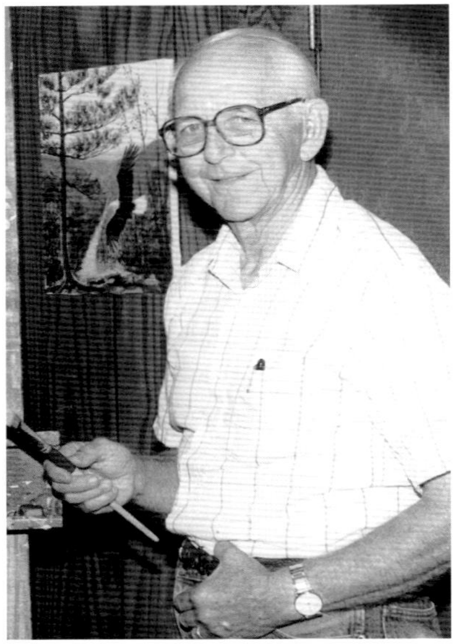

JACK CUPPER
1920-
"The Self-Taught Artist"

Photo Courtesy of Jack Cupper

Jack Cupper worked on steam locomotives for the Pennsylvania Railroad, was a radio broadcast engineer, an amateur radio operator and a self-taught artist for many years before he decided to start selling his paintings. By then, the Pennsylvania native was looking toward retirement, and eventually he chose Fredericksburg.

Tyrone, Pennsylvania, a town of 6000 in the Allegheny Mountains where Jack was born February 4, 1920, is still his second home. It always will be. But it is Fredericksburg where he and his wife, Carol, live most of the year, and where he paints Hill Country landscapes and historic German houses.

The youngest of five children, Cupper was born with a desire to draw. Growing up, he had an uncle who had lost a leg in a railroad accident and would often set Jack on his knee, propped by a wooden leg, and draw on pieces of wrapping paper. His sketches of dogs were so skillfully done that Jack, then a young boy, wanted to draw also. With this beginning, art became part of his life.

It was only a part, however. He grew up in the years of the "Great Depression," and Jack had to work. When he was 14, he delivered newspapers to earn money to buy a bicycle. In the back yard of his home, he had a small zoo where he kept rabbits, chickens, groundhogs, chipmunks, pigeons, dogs, ducks and a skunk. He supplemented his funds for animal feed by selling chickens to neighbors.

Art was a hobby, rather than a profession, as Cupper grew to manhood, although he made many paintings which he gave to his family and friends. It was not until he was in his forties that the turning point in his artistic development took place. In 1964 Cupper studied art at Elizabethtown College. From then on, he began to paint in earnest. He estimates that he did more than 600 paintings, selling some and giving away the others.

Sales were hardly enough to support him, however. A ham radio operator since his youth, he had a natural interest in electronics, and was employed in a civilian job in electronics at a nearby Air Force Base. That work would bring him to Kelly Air Force Base in San Antonio in 1966 and finally to Fredericksburg.

The move to Fredericksburg was an accident. In 1976, ready to retire from his Air Force job, he and his wife, Carol, decided they wanted to live in the Texas Hill Country. Llano was their first choice and they drove there to look at some property.

They decided it was not what they wanted and took Highway 16 back toward San Antonio. Their car broke down and had to be towed into Fredericksburg. The driver mentioned that he owned a house on Austin Street that was for sale. They took a look, liked it and it has been their home since.

Once settled in Fredericksburg, Cupper started painting with a will. Later he taught art at Williamsport Community College, Mansfield University, and at his

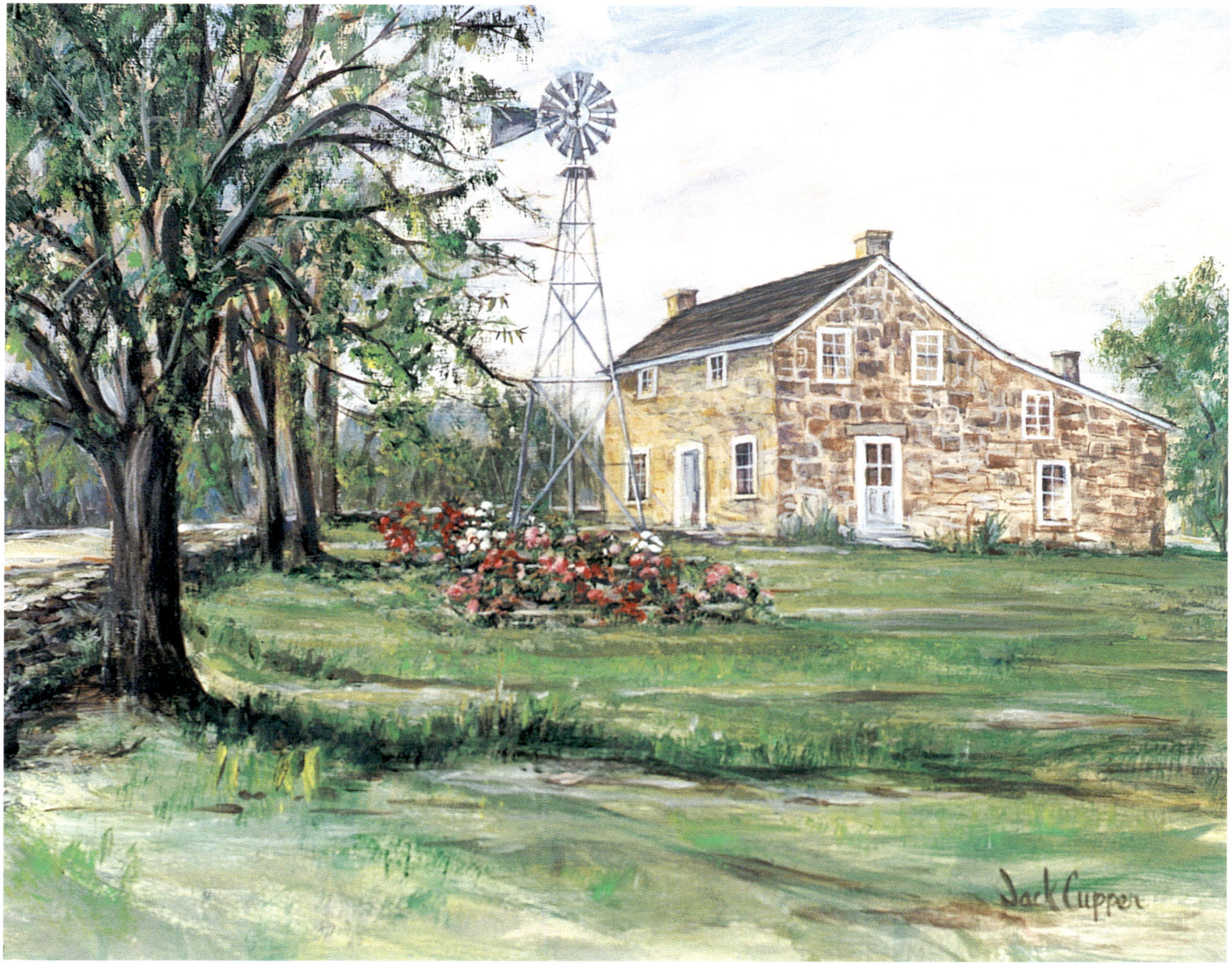

"THE RUFF HOUSE" 1973
BY JACK CUPPER
16" X 20" ACRYLIC
From the Collection of
Jeanette and Daniel Schneider

studio, all in Pennsylvania. He also taught classes for aspiring artists in the Hill Country, teaching primarily in acrylics and oils, and offered a workshop on the technique of making quick sketches of the outdoors around Fredericksburg.

Cupper started painting Hill Country landscapes and historic Fredericksburg buildings, including one of the Ruff House which won widespread acclaim. Many of the *fachwerk* homes in town also were his models. Soon his paintings were in great demand. Earlier he had exhibited in Pennsylvania and the Arnot Art Museum in Elmira, New York. Now he was being asked to exhibit in Fredericksburg, Kerrville, San Antonio and Abilene.

Jack's experience selling newspapers and chickens as a youngster had also taught him some of the tricks of marketing. Buyers like to know something of the artists whose works they buy, and shows and exhibitions aren't always enough. While living in San Antonio, he accidentally hit on an idea which made him known throughout the area.

For several years, he had donated a painting annually to KLRN, the public television station, to sell at an annual fund-raising auction. One year he was so busy that he had forgotten to produce a work for the fund drive. When the station called, he had to say "no."

Then came the idea. Why not have a professional artist show how he produced a painting from start to finish? The station liked the idea and Jack did his painting live on TV in one evening. Not only did the finished painting sell, but the idea caught on so well with the TV viewers that the station asked him to repeat the performance for several years.

Although painting and travel in their motor home occupy much of the Cuppers' time, he also writes. He does a column, "Painting Along with Jack," in the Tyrone newspaper. Earlier his column was published weekly for several years in the former Fredericksburg *Radio-Post*. The Texas column featured Hill Country paintings, descriptions of how they were produced, as well as the history and description of the location or building. He also writes poetry. One of his poems has been published in the National Library of Poetry's 1994 collection *Reflections of Light*.

Jack, who loves music, frequently sings his favorite folk songs, while being accompanied by his wife, Carol on the violin. Years earlier he sang in glee clubs, church choirs and often sang "Barber Shop" style with co-workers from Kelly Air force Base who were with the San Antonio Chordsmen. Nowadays, because of a hearing problem, he sings only with Carol or close friends.

Now, when he isn't busy at his easel or his ham radio, Cupper may be writing some poetry or attending meetings of the Sierra Club or the Audubon Society. He and Carol are avid environmentalists and bird watchers.

In fact, it is nature and conservation that is the basis for his work.

"My reason for painting is to remind all people that only natural beauty is real beauty," he says. "There are those who believe that man is destined to destroy himself, but I believe that he is seeing his errors more clearly and is gradually turning back to nature. One day he will guard and nurture that which is left with a fervor yet unknown."

Even though he has studied with some fine artists and excellent teachers, Jack professes to be mainly a self-taught artist who paints in all mediums, with no preference. Painting, he says, makes him feel better---more alert and ready to face any encounter. Through painting, he feels that he gets creative mental stimulation, in addition to the physical exercise of walking to interesting painting sites.

Critics call his work "semi-impressionistic." He says of it:

"I paint in a free, spontaneous manner because it pleases me and allows the viewers to involve themselves in my paintings."

Apparently viewers do just that. Cupper's paintings hang in homes, offices and private collections all around the USA and in several foreign countries.

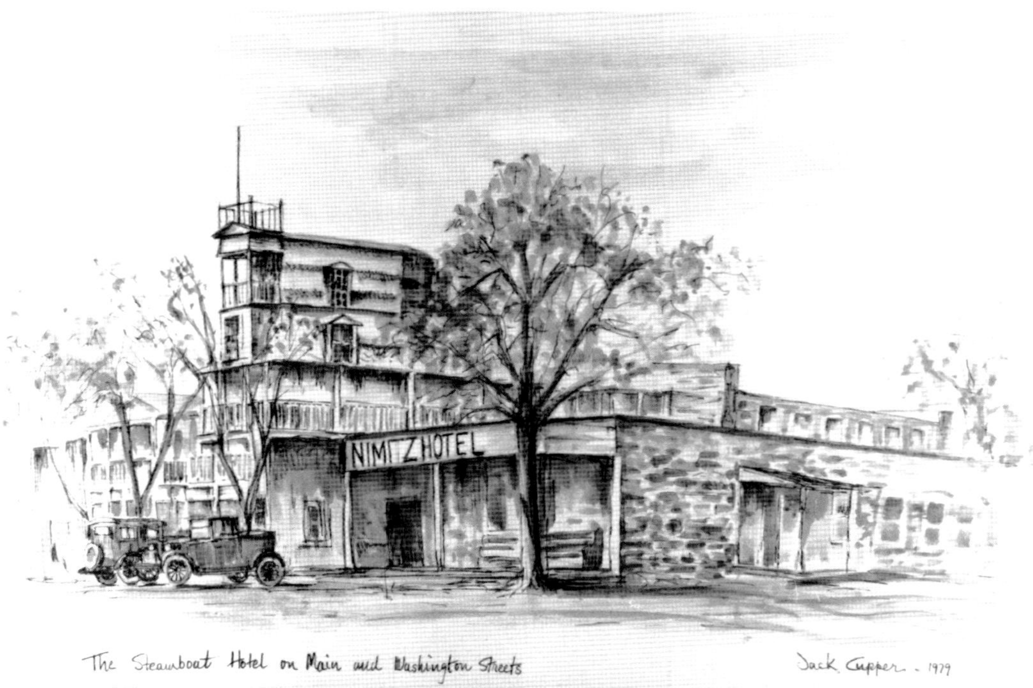

"THE STEAMBOAT HOTEL ON MAIN AND WASHINGTON STREETS" 1979
BY JACK CUPPER
11" X 17 1/4" WATERCOLOR
Courtesy of Jack Cupper

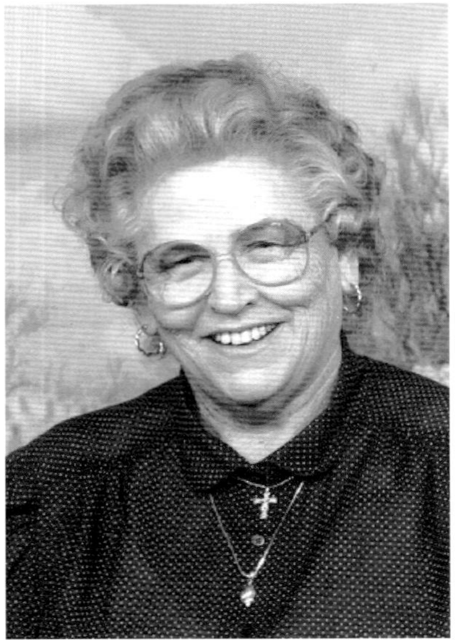

IRENE KLEIN
1921-
"The Artist Who Dreamed"

Photo Courtesy of Irene Klein

A dream that came true, one that didn't, and the San Antonio International Airport all played a role in giving Fredericksburg one of its best-known artists.

When Irene Kunz was growing up in the White Oak community in Gillespie County, she dreamed of two things---that she would one day become an artist and that she would never marry a farmer. At the time, of course, she couldn't know that an airport 75 miles away would also play an important role in whether or not those dreams would come true.

The granddaughter of German immigrants, she was born March 27, 1921 to Mr. and Mrs. Louis Kunz, Sr. Her father was a farmer and she grew up working in the family cotton fields, a job with which she never became enamored. Her distaste for field work inspired her to pray that she would someday find a husband who shared her dislike for the farm.

As a child she also knew that art had a special appeal. She dreamed of the day when she would see her signature on a painting that she had created herself.

The possibility of that dream coming true seemed remote. Her parents objected to her even thinking of art as a career. They felt that a woman's role was to be a wife and mother.

"Put those things out of your mind," her parents repeatedly told her. "That art stuff won't buy you a blanket to keep your babies warm."

It seemed even more unlikely that she would escape marriage to a farmer. Three miles down the road from the Kunz place, a handsome fellow named Otto Klein also was growing up. In 1938, when she was 17, she and Otto were married. Despite her dream, Irene had married a farmer.

She was delighted, however, to discover that Otto wanted to escape the farm, too. The couple moved to San Antonio. For 20 years, Otto worked as an auto mechanic and Irene took in sewing to help out with family finances. Later she opened a bridal consultant business which allowed her at least some outlet for her natural artistic talents. She helped brides plan every aspect of their wedding from the food served at the reception to the gown they chose.

By then, Irene's art career seemed only a remote dream, especially after Otto started his own auto repair business. She was busy raising a family of two sons and two daughters. But when the oldest daughter (the last of the children to marry) became a bride in 1970, Irene decided to act. She asked Otto if she could spend $25 to buy some paints and brushes.

He reluctantly agreed, although he was no more enthusiastic about her ambition than her parents had been decades earlier. Irene, however, had a plan.

She knew that two things were necessary if she was to become a successful artist. First, she would have to sketch or paint every day, including an occasional Sunday. And second, she had to find somebody to teach her what art was about.

The second objective took awhile. Over time she managed to participate in workshops with several renowned artists, including John McClusky and Dalhart Windberg. She decided not to stay with one teacher very long---she didn't want her work influenced too much by a single artist.

She learned something from each. Audrey Montgomery showed her how to mix paints. From A.D. Greer, she learned tips on style and the use of color. Bill Berrick taught the use---and control---of acrylics.

On her own, she decided to adopt the style of the Old Masters. And she decided to concentrate her efforts on landscapes of the Hill Country where she grew up.

Meanwhile, Otto was understanding but still not enthusiastic about her work. Once she had images on canvas, however, she wanted them to be seen. She began exhibiting them at San Antonio's famed Starving Artists show along the River Walk and *La Villita*. She had passed her 51st birthday in 1972 when the bonanza hit. In one day with the Starving Artists she sold every painting she had and came home with $400!

Otto was convinced. He became her "agent," driving her wherever she wanted to exhibit, setting up the paintings and helping her record sales. For four years---until 1976---she was a regular at the Starving Artists shows. To make sure she had a good spot to exhibit, Otto would set up as early as 3 A.M.

Now the San Antonio International Airport entered Irene's world. On the walls of the long passageways from the terminals to the boarding gates, the airport leases space to artists. There is a proviso: An artist who fails to make a sale in three months is out. Irene tried it and hit a home run!

For 13 consecutive years her paintings were offered for sale on the walls in the airport exhibit areas. Travelers from all over the world took her work home with them. Prominent collections in Germany, Japan and Venezuela include her paintings.

Not content with this success, the Kleins took to the road. For five years, they traveled the country. Wherever they went, her paintings sold. She was asked to show in major exhibitions. Commissions began to come in from all over. In 1978, they returned to the family farm in Fredericksburg and she has painted and taught without interruption since.

Today Irene paints in watercolor, acrylic, pastels and oils. She prefers oils, however. She specializes in landscapes because she knows the land from close contact, saying she got the feel of it by stumping her toes on rocks and running into cactus plants.

Most of her paintings are "made up" scenes, incorporating objects that are real. She likes for her work to tease the viewer's imagination--"where have I seen

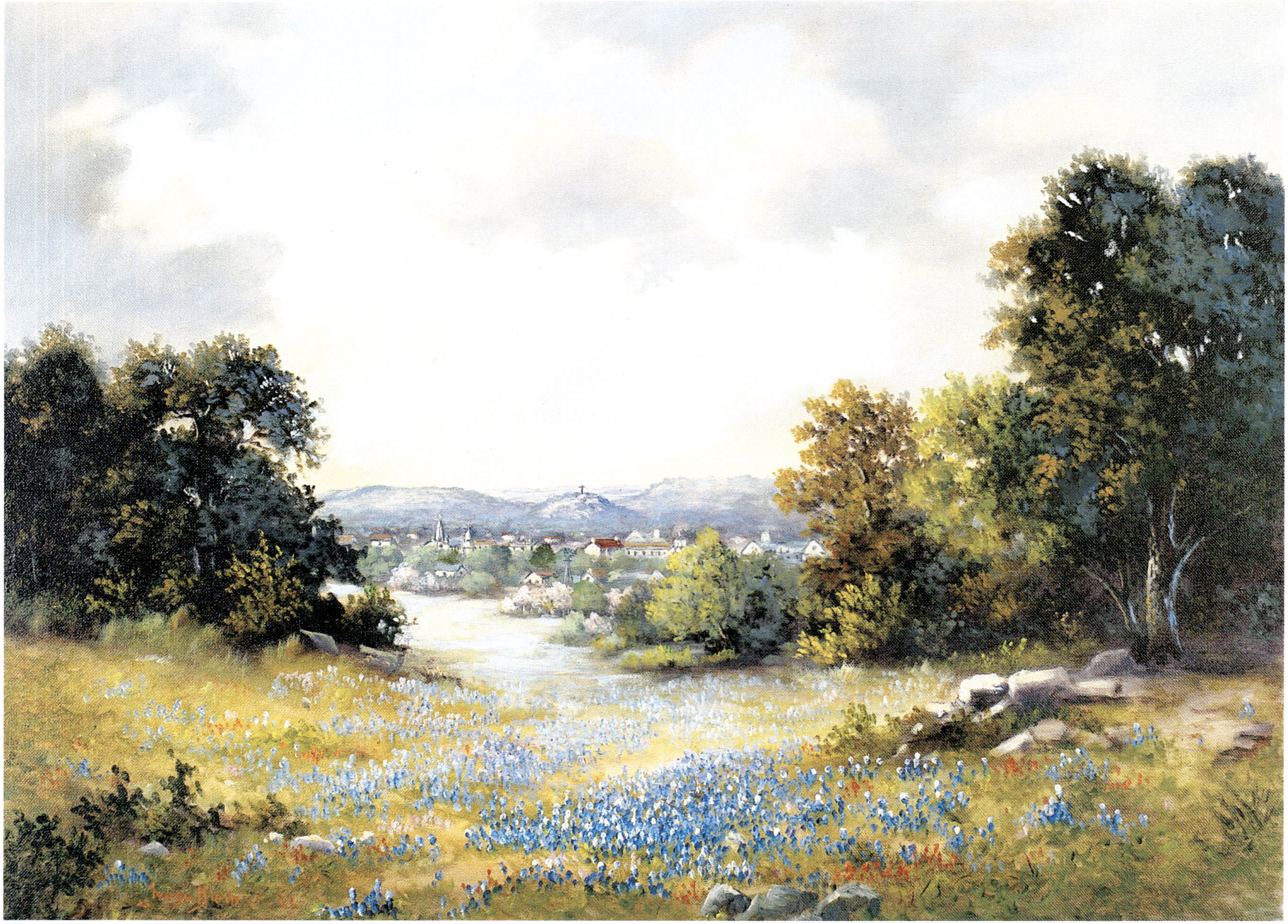

UNTITLED (DISTANT VIEW OF FREDERICKSBURG)
BY IRENE KLEIN
18" X 24" OIL ON CANVAS
From the Collection of
John and Anne Kracht

that house before?"

Irene credits San Antonio International Airport not only for helping her succeed as an artist, but for their return to Fredericksburg to live.

Otto's auto repair business was adjacent to the airport. Growth of the city and the increased air traffic made expansion of the airport necessary, and the city took the land where his business was located. Rather than find another location, they decided to retire to the farm here where she was born and grew up. The "starving artist" and the "starving mechanic" were back home at last.

"It was God's way," Irene says simply.

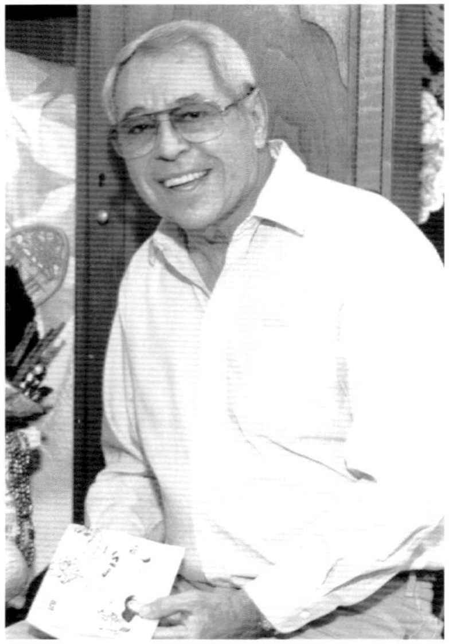

LEE ETHEL
1926-1992
"The People's Artist"

Photo Courtesy of Betty Ethel

Lee Ethel began as a designer, became nationally-known as an illustrator and ended his career as one of Texas' best-known and most respected painters.

He called his work "contemporary primitive, for lack of a better description". Critics praised his portraits, pastorals and still lifes as "bold, yet sensitive---vigorous, yet subtle." And while he didn't start painting until he was in his forties, his works today hang in museums, corporate and private collections and homes throughout the United States, and in Mexico, Europe and Japan.

Leland D. Ethel was born December 1, 1926, in Hydro, Caddo County, Oklahoma. He became a Texan when he was 12 and the family moved to Miami (pop. 660), Roberts County, in the northeastern Panhandle.

It was hardly a place to inspire a youngster toward an art career. The population was sparse---less than one person per square mile in the vast county. Ranching and wheat farming were the principal sources of income and the youth who stayed on after finishing high school usually followed these occupations. Lee, however, had known from early childhood that he wanted to be an artist of some sort. Fortunately, his fifth grade school teacher recognized his talent and encouraged him. She arranged for him to attend high school art classes long before he was ready for his freshman year.

When Lee graduated from high school, World War II was still in progress. He joined the Army and spent 18 months in specialized engineering training at Oklahoma A&M University. When he was released by the military, he joined the advertising staff of the *Pampa Daily News*. Designing ads for a small town newspaper was, at least, a start in his career. The experience convinced him that he wanted to be an illustrator.

He went to Los Angeles, enrolled in the L.S. Art Center and worked part time in the art department of the Broadway Department Stores. He discovered that he liked design better than drawing and began to specialize in that field.

While in California, Lee had visitors from home--his sister and her husband, and a fourth generation Texas lass named Betty McElroy, whom he had met earlier while she was teaching school in his hometown of Miami. At the end of the two-week vacation, Betty stayed on--she and Lee had decided to get married.

In 1948, the advertising manager of A. Harris & Co. of Dallas showed up in L.A. looking for talent, saw some of Lee's work and hired him as art/production manager of that famous store. He stayed with A. Harris for a year, then branched out. He spent the next 25 years working with various advertising agencies and an art studio. He also free-lanced his work.

During this period, Lee's work was versatile. He designed book jackets for publishers and illustrated calendars. Later, after the Ethels had moved to Fredericksburg, Lee did the illustrations for a book on Thanksgiving published by

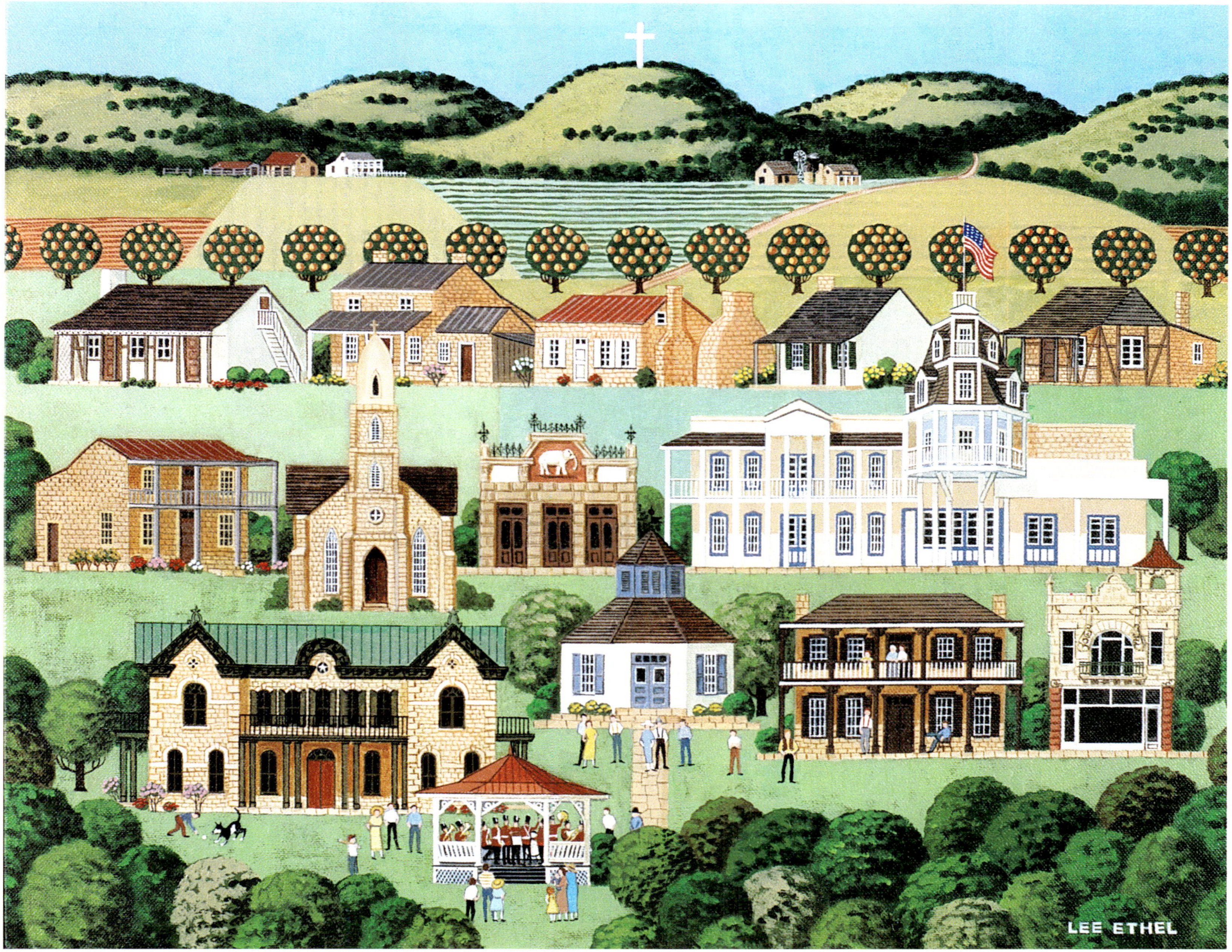

"SUNDAY AFTERNOON IN FREDERICKSBURG" 1992
BY LEE ETHEL
14" X 18" ACRYLIC ON CANVAS
From the Collection of Betty Ethel

Houghton, Mifflin, and designed the jacket for a volume by Leon Hale, the well-known Texas columnist.

In the late 1960's Lee started painting with oil on canvas. His works included many portraits. In the 1970's, he switched to using acrylic because he developed an allergic reaction to oil paint. Highly detailed, his paintings had a stylized approach, showing the strong composition derived from his years of experience in the field of graphic art and design. Although he was formally trained as a commercial artist, Ethel was essentially self-taught as a painter.

He opened a gallery in Dallas, not only to sell his own paintings, but also the works of more than 30 other well-known artists and craftsmen in the Southwest.

For a period, Lee served on the staff of *The Episcopal Churchman*, a publication of the Episcopal Diocese of Dallas. During that time, the publication was named the best of its kind in the nation.

Talented in music as well as art, Lee always sang in church choirs, and as a youth and young man, was often soloist at special services.

Ethel grew up a Methodist, but joined the Episcopal Church in 1960. From then until his death, he devoted much of his time and talent to publications of the denomination. When Fredericksburg's St. Barnabas Episcopal published an illustrated directory of its members, a painting which Lee had done of the church was used on the cover. When St. Barnabas women produced a best-selling cookbook called *Flavors of Fredericksburg*, he did the cover painting and all of the illustrations throughout.

In 1974, Lee and Betty bought and began restoring the old Carl Henke home on the corner of Llano and Travis.

By the time the Ethels moved to Fredericksburg in 1979, his paintings already were well-known. Almost immediately he began to capture the spirit of his new home on canvas. His subjects ranged from the city's pioneer homes to groupings of historic buildings. The paintings were an immediate success. People came from all over to buy an Ethel original or print of historic Fredericksburg.

Despite the success of his painting, Lee also continued to do some advertising art. The posters and bottle labels of Oberhellman Winery were designed by Ethel. The labels on *Das Peach Haus* products are his design.

He was known as "the backbone" of the Pedernales Creative Arts Association, the local group that promotes dozens of arts and crafts. When the PCAA started its famed *Oktoberfest* in the 1980's, it was Ethel who supervised most of the work of setting up and taking down the festival's booths, tents and other paraphernalia.

His experience in design did much to help make *Oktoberfest* an event that now draws up to 30,000 visitors to Fredericksburg each Fall. He designed the logo, the advertising posters and the T-shirts that have become items prized by collectors.

Painting was his life, but Lee and Betty found time for a variety of activities away from his easel. He loved aquatic sports and excelled at water-skiing. They collected and restored antiques. He was a Civil War buff and an avid genealogist, tracing his ancestry back to the American Revolution and beyond. He was a life member of the Gillespie County Historical Society, serving as director, treasurer and docent.

A warm friendly man with a magnetic personality and Sinatra-like good looks, Lee counted his friends in the hundreds. He once told an interviewer that, aside from painting, his interests were "yard, people, beer and relaxing, but not in that order."

Lee loved Fredericksburg and the Hill Country and never regretted leaving the big cities where he had spent so much of his life. On one of his brief trips back to Dallas, he quipped to a friend: "My only reason to come to town is to borrow money!"

As a designer, illustrator, painter and interpreter of an era, Ethel was "the people's artist." His nostalgic paintings reflect his genius. A "folk artist" in the best sense of that word, his pure, simple, almost photographic approach to his subjects portrays a stable, happy, less complicated world of yesteryear.

His impressions of the architecture and people of the past, rendered in bright colors, warm the heart and evoke memories of the kind of world that only a few artists, like Ethel and Norman Rockwell, have been able to capture.

Lee died December 2, 1992. He is buried in the columbarium, surrounded by the wisteria, giant oaks and historic buildings that he loved, in the church yard of St. Barnabas Episcopal in Fredericksburg.

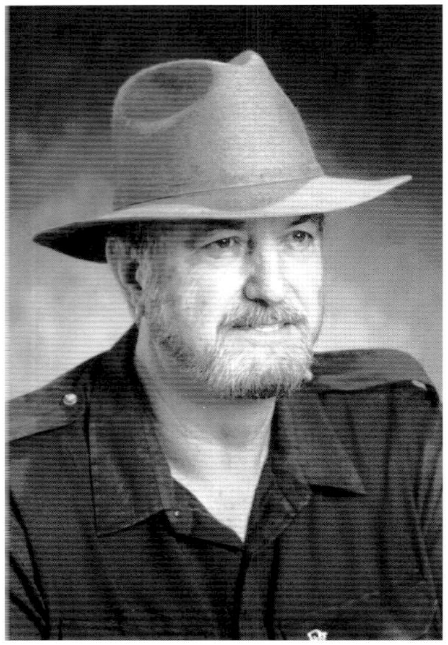

CHARLES BECKENDORF
1930-
"The Naturalist Artist"

Photo By Marc Bennett

"Fine art is that in which the hand, the head and the heart go together."

Almost a century and a half after famed London critic John Ruskin wrote this description of what he believed necessary for the creation of lasting art, his words aptly describe the work of a man who has become one of Texas' most recognized names in art. He is, as one friend observed, "the ultimate contradiction---a successful artist."

Any connoisseur who has seen a Charles Beckendorf painting or print (and almost three-quarters of a million of them hang today in every corner of the civilized world) or one of his eight books on Texas and Texas wildlife will agree that his art has an added dimension. Certainly he is a first-rate technician with brush and pencil. However, it is his additional talents as a naturalist, historian and writer which show through his paintings and drawings and sets them above most contemporary art.

In his art he demonstrates his broad knowledge of the physiology of the animals, birds and reptiles that he draws or paints. He obviously has a deep and abiding affection for them and he puts these feelings not only into his paintings, but also into beautiful prose in his books.

"My first interest in animals, or at least my first memory, is of feeding chickens and guinea-fowl on hard dirt surfaces around our house and barns. My first chores were feeding and watering livestock, and my first unpleasant experiences came when they were sold or slaughtered."

When he paints people and places, the naturalist becomes the meticulous historical researcher. His research is accurate and precise and his knowledge of the history and geography of this state is greater than many academicians. He owns one of the largest private Texana libraries extant.

Charles Beckendorf's family came to Texas in 1846. His grandchildren are not only sixth generation Texans, but are also sixth generation residents of Fredericksburg; his wife's family was one of the first to settle here in 1846.

Born in 1930, Beckendorf grew up on a small South Texas farm near the town of Mathis in San Patricio County. His father worked for a pipeline company; his mother was a concert pianist who also taught piano and voice lessons. Neither encouraged their only child to consider art as a career.

Even though Charles drew and painted on everything he could get his hands on as a youngster, he had no notion of becoming an artist either. Art wasn't taught in the public schools in Mathis.

Beckendorf tells of his interest in art during his school years in an excerpt from one his books, *Charles Beckendorf, Texas Wildlife*:

"In primary school I spent my time drawing rather than adhering to the recommended curriculum, and I drew the three things I admired the most: animals, airplanes and girls. Teachers said they liked my animal drawings; they were

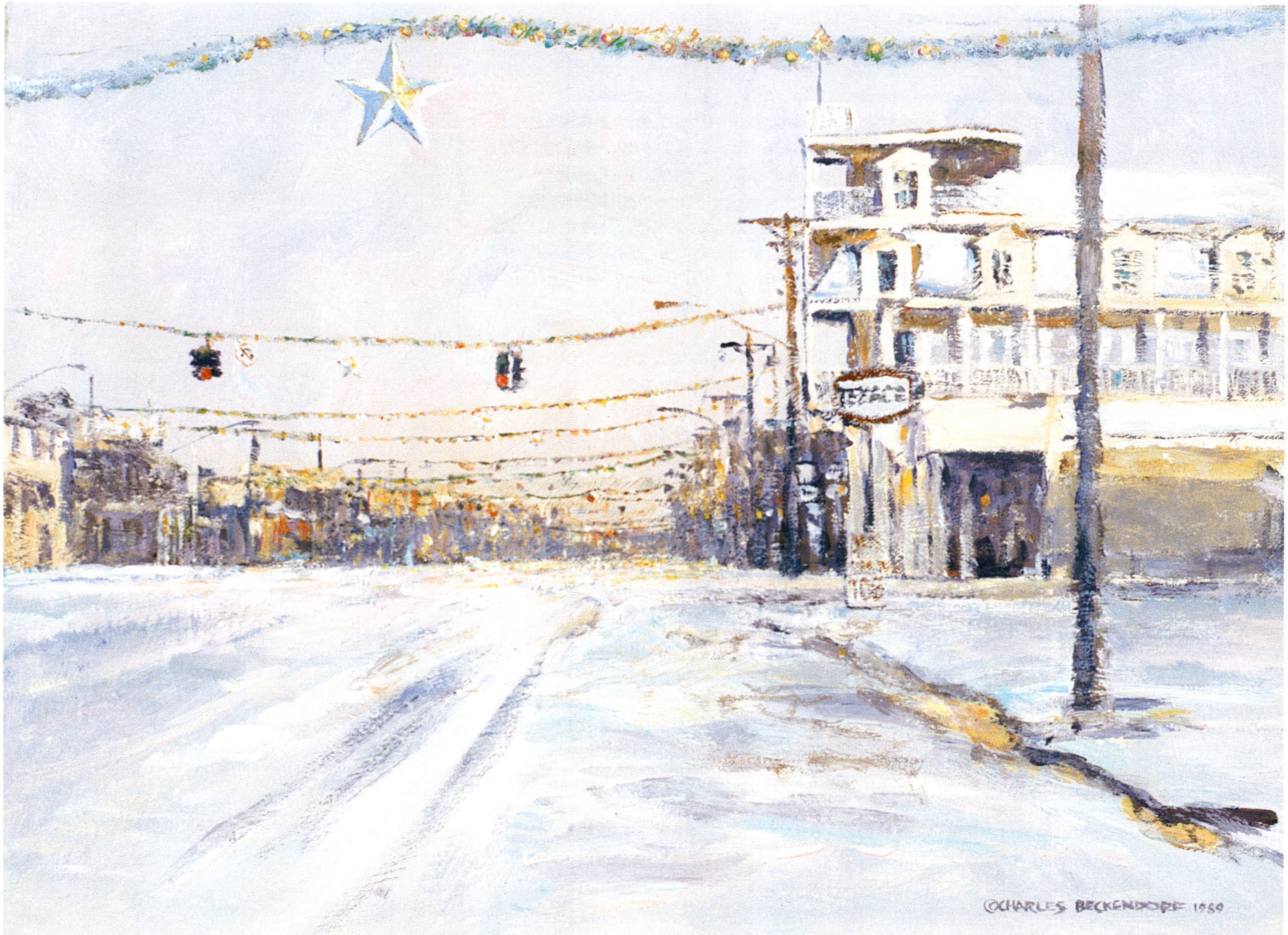

"MAIN STREET CHRISTMAS"
BY CHARLES BECKENDORF
12" X 16" ACRYLIC ON CANVAS
From the Collection of
Dawn Beckendorf

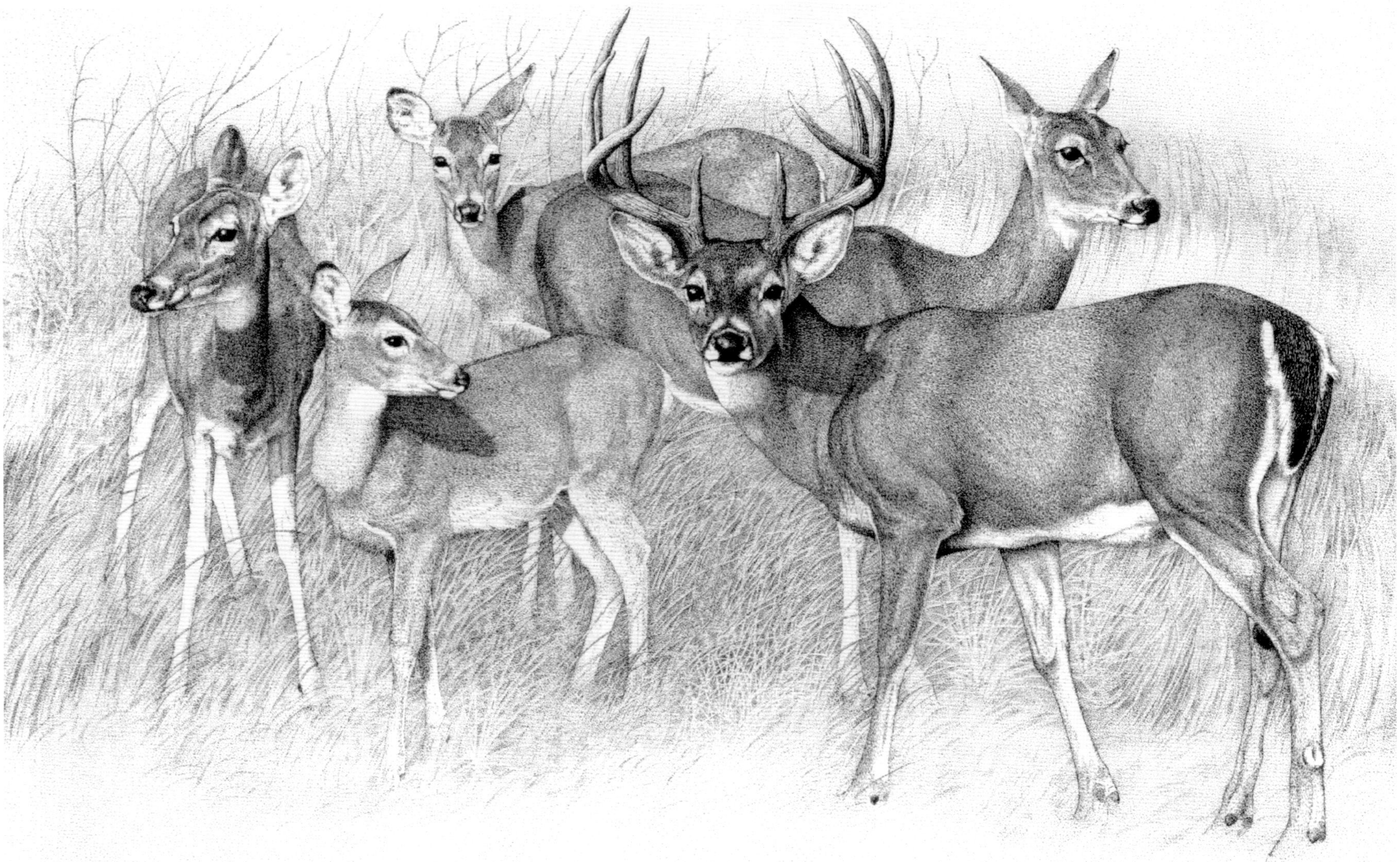

"WHITETAIL DEER-MASTER SERIES"
BY CHARLES BECKENDORF
18" X 28" PEN AND INK
Courtesy of
Charles Beckendorf Gallery

ambivalent toward my airplane drawings; but they became incensed with my girl drawings. I decided I had better stick with animal drawings for any public display.

"My high school years were spent in an adversarial position with teachers and school administrators who believed that day-dreaming and drawing could never produce an acceptable candidate for this or any other society. The colleges and universities I later attended also held a narrow view of those who brought their own priorities of matriculation on campus."

He attended the Mathis schools, the University of Corpus Christi and Southwest Texas State where he met his future wife Dawn Laurence, before serving with the Air Force in the Korean War. After the war he finished his degree at The University of Texas. Through it all, he studied art and drew what he saw around him.

In his youth, Beckendorf listened to stories told by Anglo and Mexican ranch hands, trappers, hunters and drifters. He met old Indian fighters, rangers and Civil War veterans, cattle barons, cotton kings and Texas oil men. He became convinced that no better heritage was ever left to anyone than the Texas landscape and its animals, and he was going to spend his life learning, drawing and painting Texas.

From the time Beckendorf enrolled in his first art course, his only goal has been to paint what people enjoy, and he has decided to concentrate on portraying his native land.

Even though he has received many honors from governments, universities and corporations, it has been when a young person has said: "My folks have had Mr. Beckendorf's art around for as long as I can remember and now that I have a place of my own, I want his art on my walls also," that Beckendorf has felt that he has received his highest honor.

Beckendorf's gallery has been in operation in Fredericksburg since 1971, before Fredericksburg became the tourist attraction it is today. The gallery is home to hundreds of his prints, latest originals, books and bronzes. Thousands of people visit yearly.

As Larry Hodge wrote in *Texas Highways*:

"One person whose name is virtually synonymous with the town (Fredericksburg) is Charles Beckendorf."

Almost 60 years since his first drawing, Beckendorf is still at it---drawing and painting pictures of what people like to see and drawing and painting pictures of which people can truly relate.

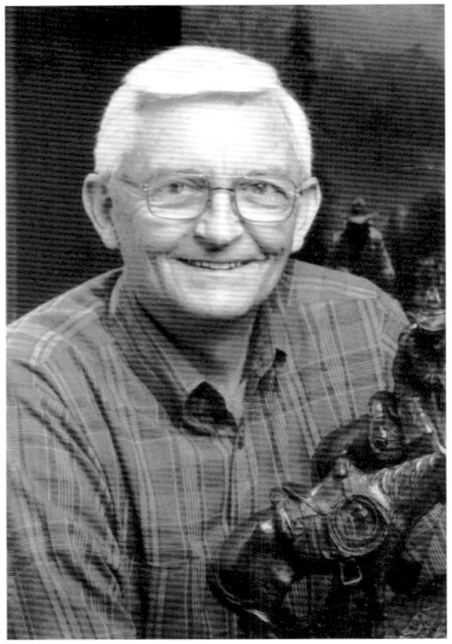

G. HARVEY
1933-
"Light in the Hills"

Photo By Marc Bennett

Gerald Harvey Jones grew up certain of two things: He wanted to be an artist and he wanted to stay in the Texas Hill Country. He succeeded on both counts.

Today his paintings hang in collections around the world and his sculptures grace homes, offices and museums. And since 1983, Fredericksburg has been his home and studio.

Born in San Antonio in 1933, he was drawing before he was old enough for kindergarten. His early sketches were mostly of horses and ranch life and bluebonnets, inspired by tales about his grandfather, one of the last cowboys to trail cattle across the Red River.

In high school, Gerald took every art course offered. However, when he enrolled in North Texas State Teachers College at Denton (now the University of North Texas), he was considering drafting and architecture as a profession. He earned a degree in Industrial Arts.

His next stop was Austin in 1957 where he taught in the junior high school, then joined the staff of The University of Texas as supervisor of Arts and Crafts in the Student Union. By then, painting had become a passion, but there was no time to work at his easel except nights and weekends. He was encouraged when he managed to sell a few paintings for $25.

One day a friend suggested that the name, Gerald Harvey Jones, didn't sound very artistic. So he dropped the "Jones", Gerald became only the initial "G" and "G. Harvey," the artist, was born. Sure enough, a local gallery took some of his work, and a few more paintings sold for $50 and up, some bringing $150.

His wife, Pat, who has always been his inspiration, encouraged him, in 1964, to go full time in art. It was a frightening decision for a young artist, but he had three things in his favor:

Talent, discipline and a wife who believed in him.

"He wanted to be an artist so badly that he just had to give it a try," Pat says.

They both agree that this decision was right. A year after starting on his own, he entered his first major art show---the prestigious Grand National Exhibition in New York. He was startled to be given the New Masters Award by the American Artists Professional League. He needn't have been---the honors and awards haven't stopped since.

John Connally, then Texas' governor, had seen the young artist's work and commissioned him to do 12 different scenes of the Connally ranch near Floresville. He presented them to governors of Mexican states. The White House staff asked Harvey to paint the LBJ birthplace, boyhood home and ranch house for the President's birthday. The President also commissioned a Harvey painting as a gift for the Prime Minister of Japan.

From then on, the name G. Harvey began to emerge in art circles around the

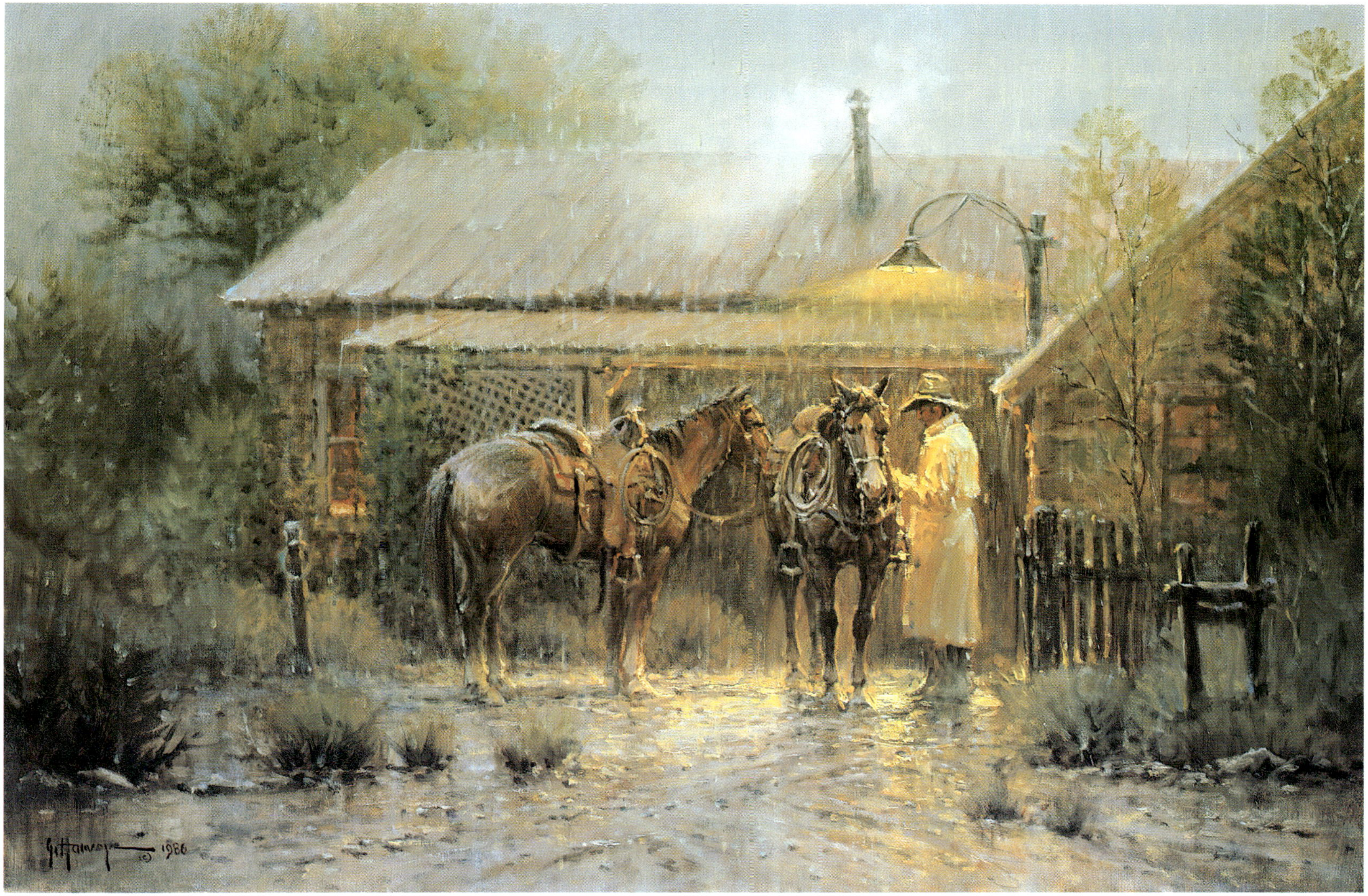

"TEXAS RANCHER"
BY G. HARVEY ©
20" X 30" OIL
From the Collection of
George S. Hinkle

nation. Today he produces some twenty paintings a year, plus several sculptures and limited edition prints. By any reckoning, he is one of America's most popular living artists.

Although he is what he calls "a grass roots Texan" and loves painting horses most of all, he does not consider himself a "cowboy artist." He paints what he knows and loves, but he no longer limits his work to a geographic area. He has painted in France, England, Russia and Washington, D.C., and Civil War battlefields have been the subjects of some of his best-known works.

In the 1992 edition of the *International Art Collector* he said: "My art is a natural extension of my heritage---of a way of life that my parents and grandparents had that our children will never see in the natural state. I am trying to conserve that atmosphere on canvas."

A shy, almost reclusive man, he admits to not liking gallery crowds or the spotlight fame brings. In one on one encounters or in small groups, however, he is warm, friendly and enjoys good talk. Both he and Pat are committed Christians and active in their local church. While they love Fredericksburg, they do spend much time traveling.

In 1991, Gerald was commissioned by the Smithsonian Institution to create 30 paintings on the history of the horse in North America for the "Seeds of Change" exhibition that commemorated the 500th anniversary of Columbus' discovery of America. It was a two-year project, involving considerable historical research.

"I had painted the horse many times in many work-related ways," he recalls. "The exhibition, however, spanned the time when the *Conquistadores* brought them to this country, how they spread across the West and into the cities and were used in oil fields and city life...It was right up my alley."

Later that same year, the National Archives hosted an evening with G. Harvey to unveil four major oil paintings he had done chronicling the Civil War. Most recently he completed a historical lithograph series titled "Symbols of the Nation" for the U.S. Treasury Historical Association. They feature the White House, the Lincoln Memorial, the Washington Monument and the Capitol.

Whether historic or Western in subject matter, it is the unusual lighting in Harvey's work that first catches the eye of the viewer. As Christine Mollring, president of the Scottsdale, Arizona, Trailside Americana Gallery that handles Harvey's work says:

"Ask anyone who has viewed a G. Harvey painting what the work's distinguishing characteristic is, and undoubtedly their response will be 'the artist's incredible ability to capture light.'"

When a San Antonio newspaper ran a feature article on the artist and his home and studio in Fredericksburg, the headline read: LIGHT IN THE HILLS.

If Harvey enjoys anything more than his family, his church and his painting, it is the historic two-story stone house that he and Pat restored in 1983-84. It was built in 1853 by Carl Weyrich, a locksmith, who had arrived with the first settlers seven years before. Since 1918, the house had been owned by the Arhelgers, another pioneer family. They were reluctant to sell the home until three generations of Arhelgers had met with Pat and Gerald to make certain that the property would be preserved.

In planning the restoration, they asked Helen Weirich, for many years the town librarian and a distant relative of the builder, to advise. With her help, and that of other experts, they took almost two years to restore the house and its spacious grounds.

The compound includes the home, a guest house and a two-story studio, where Gerald produces his paintings and sculptures. In the studio is an extensive research library. A high privacy fence of stone surrounds the grounds.

Gerald Harvey Jones says the house is both an ideal home and the perfect place to paint. He usually is in his studio by 7:30 A.M. and remains until 7 P.M. except for a short lunch break. On occasion, he has been known to nap briefly in the afternoon. And while he enjoys the long hours doing research or at his easel, he refuses to work on a deadline.

"Those about me understand, and give me the time. A painting of mine is finished when it's finished!"

Whatever the subject on his canvas may be, and however long it may take to complete it, Harvey makes one point clear:

"Everything I paint is filtered through my faith, my family, my friends, my heritage and my roots in Texas.

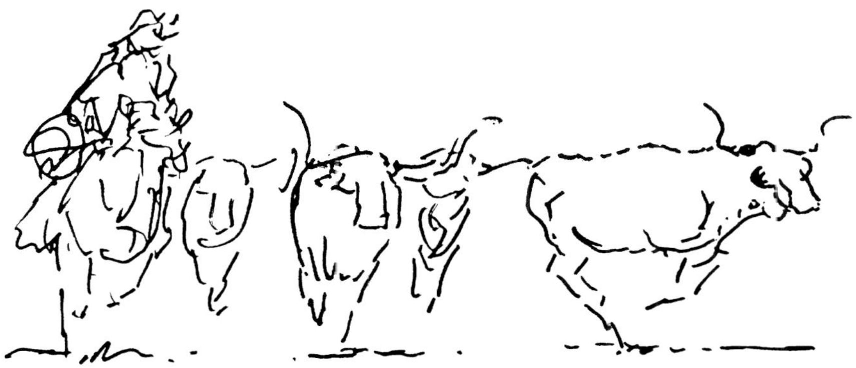

"ROUND-UP"
PENCIL SKETCH BY G. HARVEY ©
Courtesy of G. Harvey

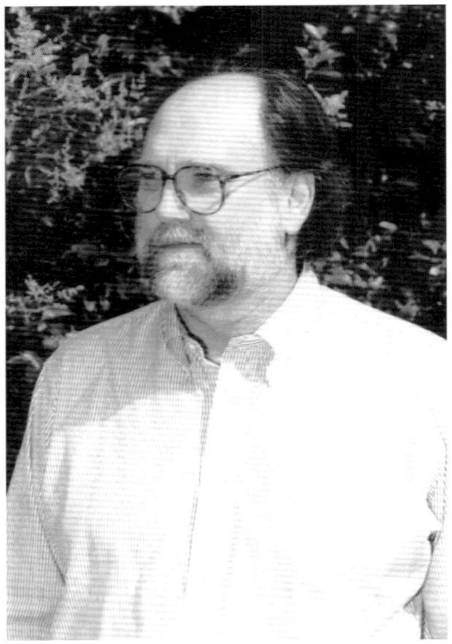

JOHN AUSTIN HANNA
1942-
"The Professional Artist"

Photo By Joe Beckendorf, Fredericksburg, Texas

An emergency appendectomy pointed John Hanna toward a successful career as an illustrator and eventually into producing paintings that have won widespread acclaim.

Whether it was the anesthesia or something else that triggered his desire to be an artist, he can't say. All he knows is that his first thoughts of art came at the age of five when he awoke from surgery in a Beaumont hospital.

From then until he entered high school, art was an on and off thing. His parents encouraged him, and didn't object when they found him, on many nights, in his bedroom drawing at 1 A.M. In middle school, he began winning a few ribbons and awards for his sketches.

Meanwhile he also had discovered a game called baseball and his interest in art took a back seat for awhile. However, in junior high and high school, he took every course available in drafting and mechanical drawing and decided he had found the career path he wanted.

The career wasn't long in coming. between his sophomore and junior years in high school, he was offered a summer job in the art department of a television station in Lubbock. It introduced him to a new avenue for his talent. when he enrolled at Texas Tech University in 1960, he already had working experience in the field of commercial art. It was during his four years at Tech that he also became aware that good commercial illustrations also could be fine art.

With his degree in Advertising Art and Design from Tech in hand, he went to Dallas where he was offered two jobs. However, a close friend, Bill Neale, who was with Tracy-Locke Advertising in Dallas, encouraged him to go to New York, so he and his wife decided to head North.

Hanna arrived in the Big Apple with the names of three prospective employers. He was dismayed to find that one had died, a second had gone out of business and the third was about to close his studio. When he tried the New York Society of Illustrators, however, his luck changed, and he was hired on the spot by Ted Bates Advertising, at that time the third largest advertising agency in the world.

After nine months, he became a TV art director and began producing some television on the side. He was making money and enjoying early success, but the work was taking him away from his first love---drawing. So he quit, and began free lancing his talents as an illustrator.

The commercial world welcomed him. He did art work for magazines like *Saga, Argosy, Car and Driver, Boating, Flying, Automobile Quarterly* and others. Book publishers like Harcourt Brace & World and Random House asked him to illustrate.

Nevertheless, the glamour of New York paled. Hanna missed his native Texas. (He was born July 11, 1942 in Beaumont.) In 1969, he moved to Dallas and

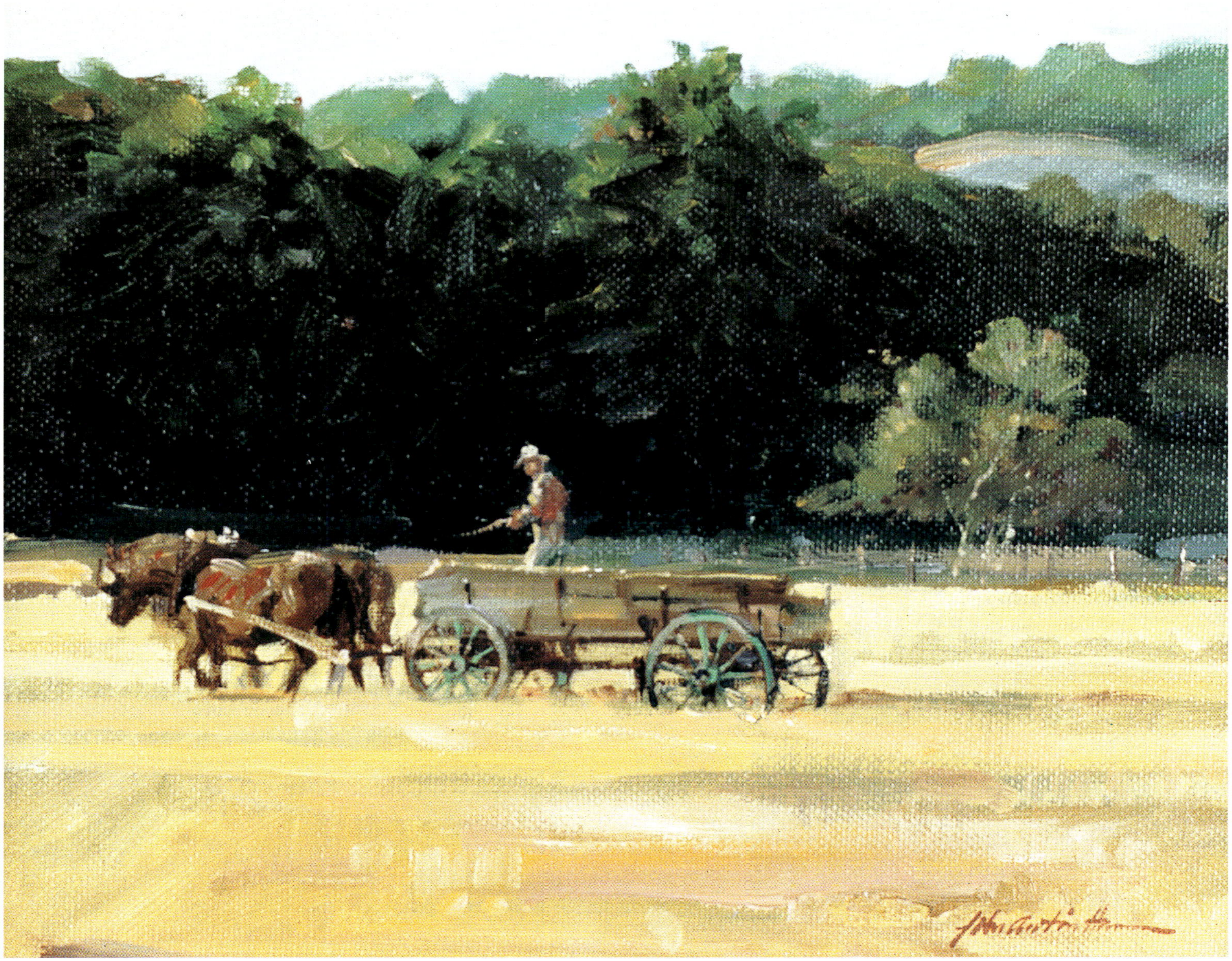

"MR. DIETZ"
BY JOHN AUSTIN HANNA
8" X 10" OIL
From the Collection of
Sherman and Valerie Durst

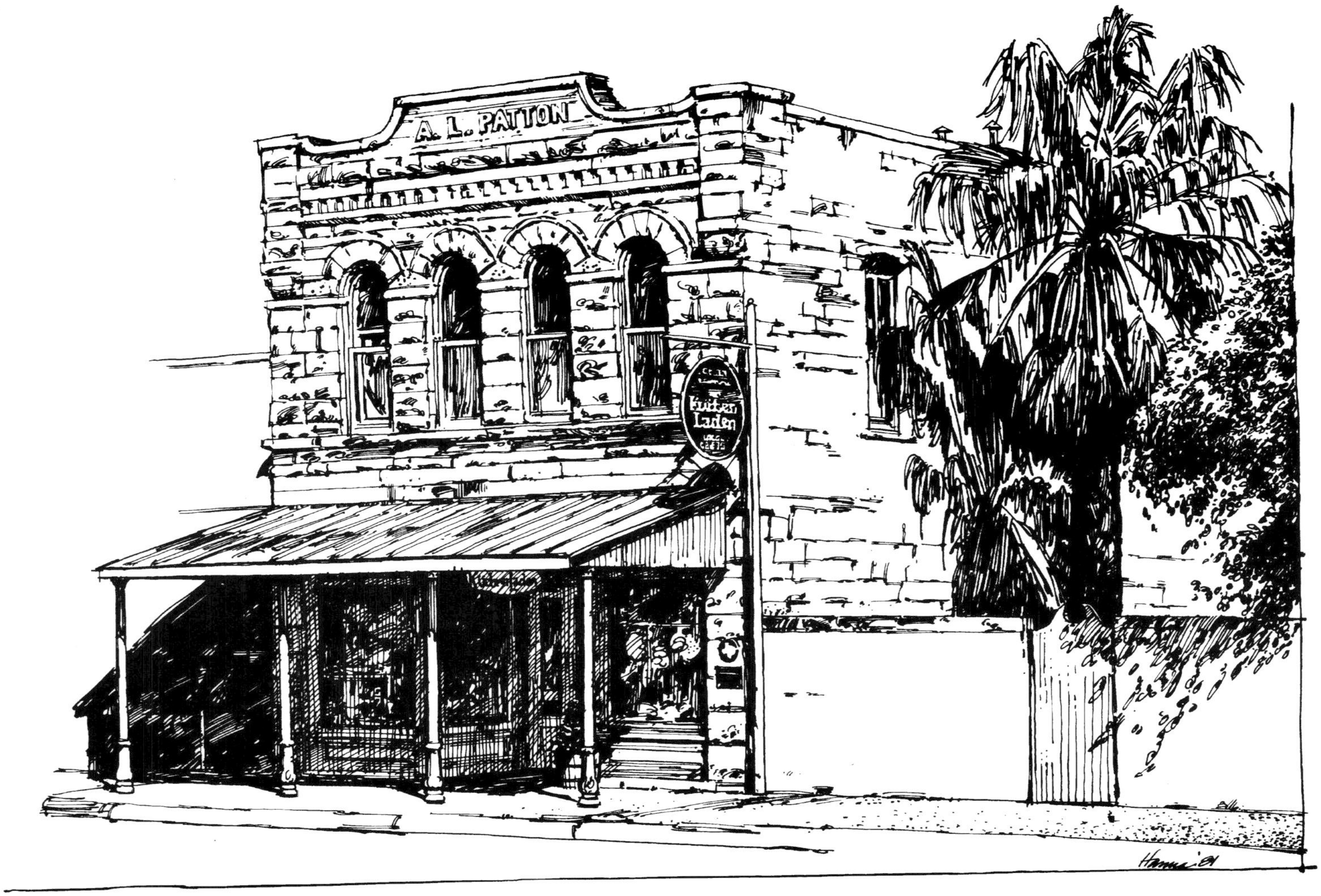

"A. L. PATTON BUILDING"
(DER KUCHEN LADEN)
BY JOHN AUSTIN HANNA
12" X 16" PEN & INK
From the Collection of
Louis and Jan Buehn

started a design and illustration studio, Point Incorporated, (later Point Communications) with Tracy-Locke Advertising. After two and a half years however, he decided to try free lancing again.

His work was once again in demand. Clients have included Phillips 66, Mobil, Texas Instruments, Rockwell-International, Zales Jewelers, Bordens, and many smaller accounts.

Hanna still was not satisfied. He was enjoying his work and making a good living, but wanted to find a new meaning in his art. In 1978, he "discovered" Fredericksburg, bought and restored a 1910 house and made the Hill Country his permanent home. He decided to paint rather than illustrate.

He rented studio space over Dooley's 5 & 10 Cent Store on Main Street and began showing his paintings at Southwest Images in Fredericksburg and the Sportsman's Gallery in Houston. At the same time, he was still receiving commissions for commercial work from Dallas and New York. He also did advertising illustrations for Fredericksburg businesses.

Then in 1985, an art director Hanna had known in New York moved to Austin to join an advertising agency there. He called John and asked if he would be interested in doing some television work. John agreed.

At the time, he was still showing his paintings in galleries in Austin, Dallas, Houston, San Antonio, Santa Fe and Ruidoso. However, the commercial work for television increased to a point where it was taking all of his time. Again, he moved away from easel painting.

By 1990, he had decided to focus all of his artistic energy on his painting. Now his work is back in galleries in Dallas; San Antonio; Scottsdale, Arizona; Carmel, California, and Jackson, Wyoming. This time, he expects to forget commercial art and continue to concentrate on his oils.

Hanna says that creating good pictures that have something to say, even to a few, is his ultimate goal. His fellow Fredericksburg artist and friend, Jack Cupper, thinks he's on the right track. In a newspaper article Cupper wrote in 1979 as a kind of personal letter to Hanna, he said:

"Your paintings show an ability far beyond the ordinary...They speak out that you know how to handle color, values and brush work in a manner that conveys maximum meaning. You do it all without finicky details. But most of all, your paintings are a thrill to look at because they have life."

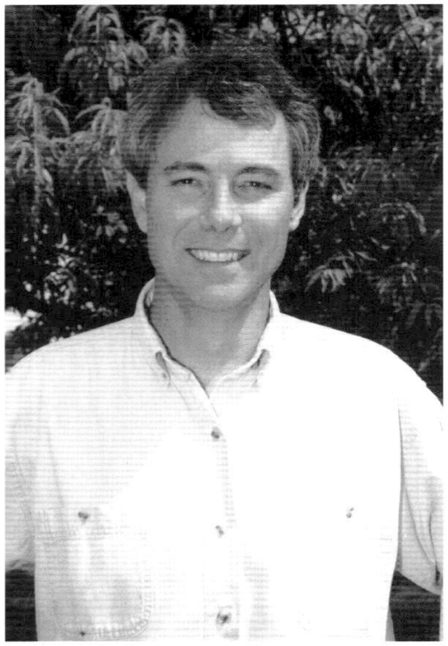

MARK HAWORTH
1952-
"The Publicist Painter"

Photo By Joe Beckendorf, Fredericksburg, Texas

Mark Haworth, one of Fredericksburg's youngest painters to gain national prominence, and Seth Eastman, the soldier-artist stationed here when the settlement was in its swaddling-clothes a century and a half ago, have much in common.

Eastman's 15 sketches and paintings made in 1848 introduced the new German village on the Texas frontier to the rest of the world. Haworth's murals and smaller paintings of the Fredericksburg of today have been seen and admired by thousands from coast to coast.

Mark didn't plan it that way. A representational impressionist, he discovered Fredericksburg as a favorite subject after he moved here in 1983. In residence less than a year, he was commissioned by Texas American Bank (now Bank One) to do a 3x12-foot mural for the local bank's lobby. It would depict the town of Fredericksburg.

It was a challenging assignment. To get the exact perspective that he wanted, Haworth rented a "cherry-picker" that elevates workmen on electrical and telephone lines. He stationed it atop the hill where the Windcrest sub-division stands a mile south of Main Street. Standing on the "cherry-picker" at this, and other locations, he photographed views of oak trees and a peach orchard and of Main Street, seen through the light of a mid-summer afternoon.

Then he went into town and shot the facades of all of the main historic buildings that face south. Next he drew the buildings to scale in pencil on a 12-foot length of brown paper. From the photos and drawings, he created a sketch in pastels. Then it all went on canvas.

The result was his "Fredericksburg---An Enduring Heritage." It's seen by hundreds of bank visitors daily. Postcards of the central portion have been sent throughout the country by the Chamber of Commerce.

Haworth's mural that is seen regularly by the most people, however, is in the lobby of Frost Bank in downtown Austin. The 4x12-foot oil shows the skyline of Austin as seen from the UT Tower and the Capitol south to Palmer Auditorium.

In 1989, the J.C. Penney Co. was running a series of national advertisements using paintings illustrating "Lone Star Lifestyles." They chose Haworth to do a 24x36-inch painting called "Fredericksburg Spring." A field of bluebonnets and an oak tree dominate the foreground and the flowers lead the viewer to a peach orchard in bloom. Beyond the orchard is a panorama of the city and the distant hills.

Thousands of readers saw the painting reproduced in full color in magazines. When the Kennedy Center in Washington, D.C., staged a "Texas Festival," Haworth's "Fredericksburg Spring" was a featured painting.

A native of Houston, Mark began drawing before he was in kindergarten. His mother was an accomplished pianist and his father an advertising executive. He was one of six children. As a child, he traveled often with his family to New York,

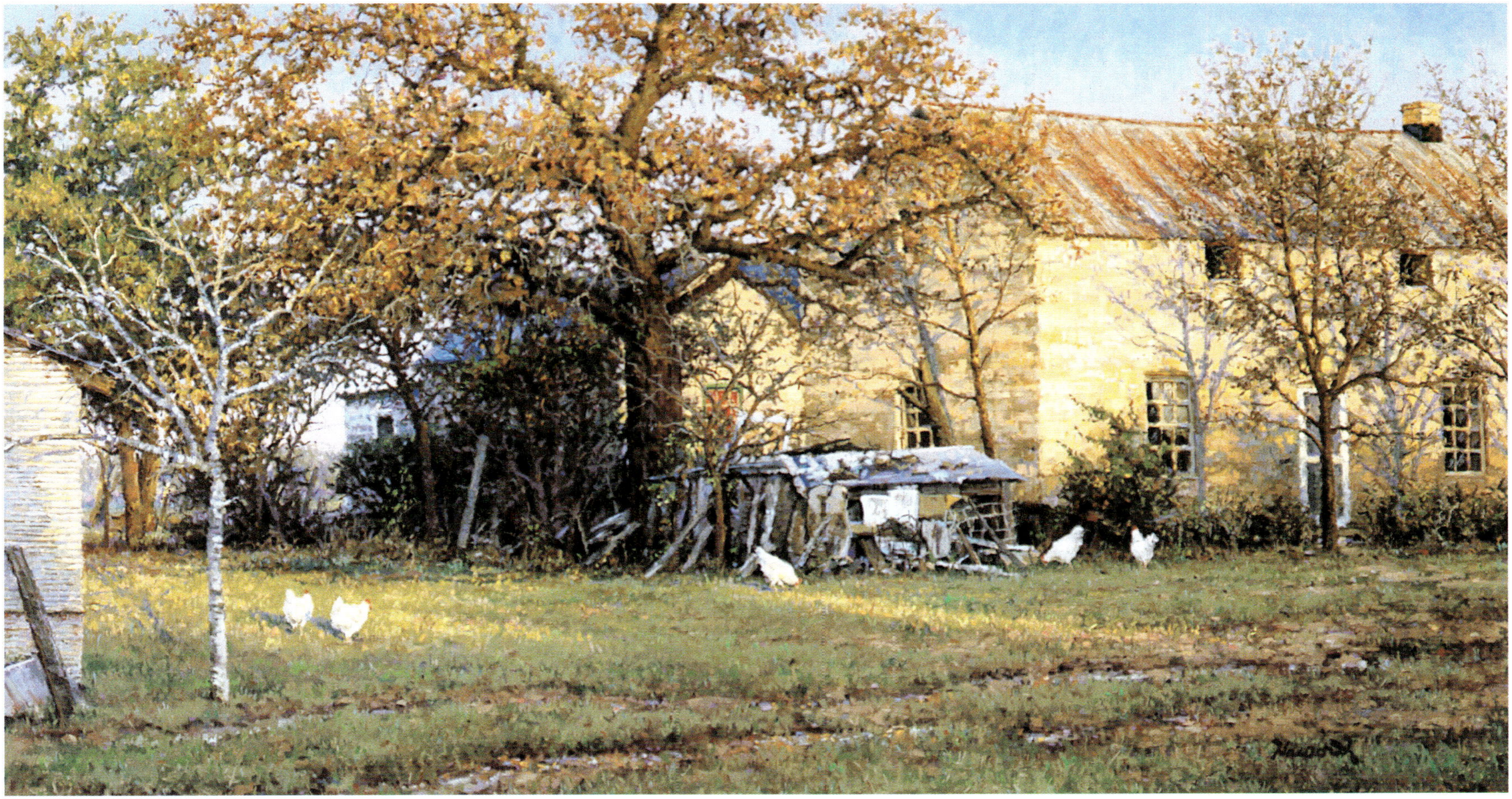

"THE CHICKEN COOP"
BY MARK HAWORTH
16" X 29" PASTEL
From the Collection of
Mark Haworth

Washington and Boston and was fascinated by visits to the major museums.

Mark took every art class available from grade through high school and was drawing and painting constantly. Once, in grade school, he was forced to borrow the janitor's mop and clean up a drawing he had made in crayon on the classroom floor. He refers to it wryly as "my first one-man show."

Music was his second love, next to art, and when he enrolled at Sam Houston State University at Huntsville, he took voice and music composition his first year instead of art. (He still plays the guitar and sings tenor with the Fredericksburg Chorale).

Haworth says he might have gone into music if he hadn't met Glenn Bahm, a nationally-known portrait painter. Bahm not only convinced him to stay with art, but hired him as an apprentice. He worked with Bahm on weekends while he was in school. In summer, he painted ten hours a day in Bahm's studio. Meanwhile he changed his major to art in his sophomore year and transferred to the University of Houston for a time. He then returned to Sam Houston University where he received a Bachelors of Fine Arts degree with honors.

Barely out of college, Mark received his first commission---to paint a different oil landscape each month for two years for Alfred Lamson, an oil man in Lafayette, Louisiana. He got another commission from Lamson to paint scenes of sandy beaches from Destin to St. George Island, Florida.

Commissions kept him financially secure, but Haworth wanted more inspiring subjects. He started to paint landscapes for gallery shows and joined the Coppini Academy of Fine Arts in San Antonio so he would have more time to paint landscapes. He was named the Academy's "Artist of the Year" in 1981.

In 1983, he married Ginny Short. Both knew Fredericksburg. He had been coming here on brief trips to paint Hill Country houses and landscapes, and like his long ago predecessor, Seth Eastman, Haworth had fallen in love with this town and the countryside. Two weeks after their marriage, Mark and Ginny decided to make it their permanent home.

Once settled in Fredericksburg, Mark decided to attend some workshops at the Cowboy Artists of America Museum in Kerrville. The workshops, taught by famous cowboy artists like Bill Moyers, Robert Pummill and Howard Terpning, are not limited to Western themes. Sharing one class was Alan Bean, the fourth man to walk on the moon. Bean paints scenes from his moon missions.

Each year, the Cowboy Artists choose five students from the class to show their work. Mark's work was shown for each of the four consecutive years that he participated.

Although he is well-known for his landscapes of Fredericksburg, Austin and other Hill Country areas, Mark occasionally paints birds. In 1989, his pastel of a moor hen wading the swamp water near Avery Island, Louisiana, was selected for the prestigious "Birds in Art" exhibit at the Leigh Yawkey Woodson Art Museum in Wausau, Wisconsin. It later toured the country for a year, showing at other art and natural history museums.

Each year since 1990 he has participated in the nation's important "Miniature" shows with one or two paintings. Entries can be no larger than 9x12-inches. Shows are at the National Museum of Wildlife Art in Jackson, Wyoming; the White Oak Gallery in Edina, Minnesota, and the Thomas Gilcrease Museum in Tulsa.

He regularly is represented in the Nita Stewart Haley Memorial Library annual art show and sale in Midland and at Texas Art Gallery in Dallas where he participates in their biannual auction and sale each Fall and Spring. He shows also at Hamdy Fine Arts in Fredericksburg. At both galleries his work hangs next to that of some of the finest representational artists in the country.

Although only in his early 40's, Haworth has won plaudits from critics throughout the country. As one wrote about his work:

"The most interesting aspect of a Haworth painting is his refusal to be a 'band-wagon' artist. He is not content to paint a typical bluebonnet scene, but must look deeper to make a more powerful statement. His challenge is in selecting landscape subject matter that sparks his interest in color and composition."

Of his own art, Haworth says:

"Art is the mirror of one's self. You can't escape that if you create artistically.

"Sometimes I hit the mark; sometimes I fail miserably. That is why the great masters, as great as their paintings may seem, are only accredited with having created a handful of truly great pieces during their lifetimes. This is why an artist is driven to keep trying again---to keep exploring and taking risks to reach new plateaus. This is the challenge that I love."

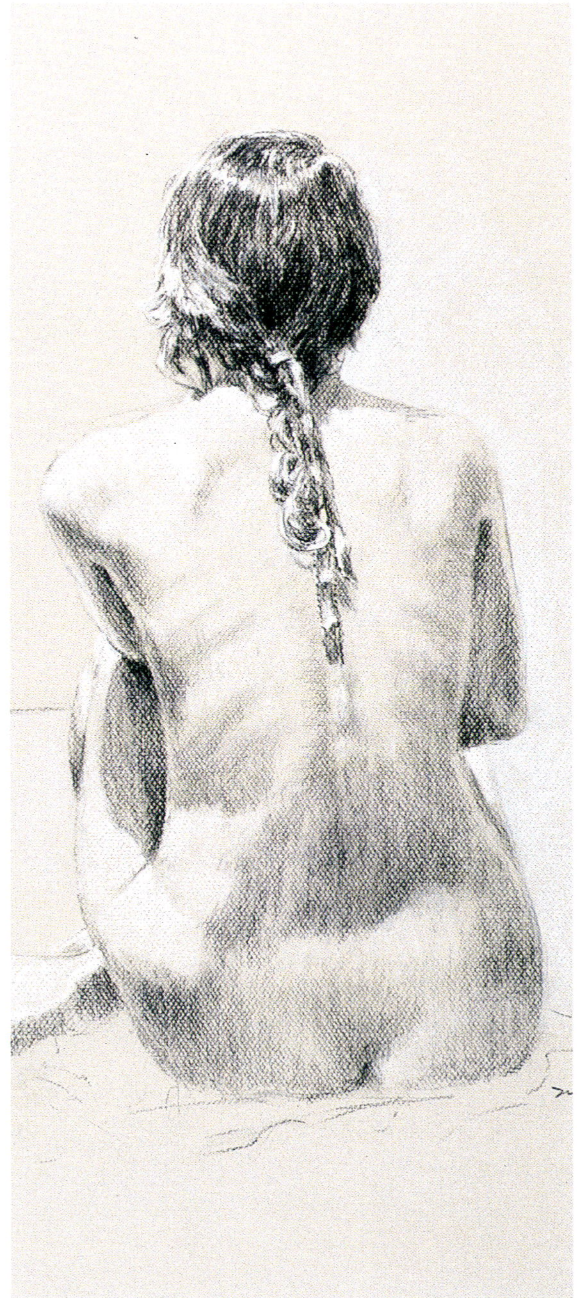

NUDE STUDY BY MARK HAWORTH
24" X 18" CHARCOAL ON PAPER
Courtesy of Mark Haworth

Index to Paintings and Drawings

Bartholmae, Onieta Merrie
"Lange's Mill", 80

Beckendorf, Charles
"Texas Longhorn", Copyright Page
Drawing-Bronze Bust of John O. Meusebach, 9
Drawing-Fredericksburg Building, 12
"Main Street Christmas", 95
"Whitetail Deer-Master Series", 96

Bierschwale, Edna Helen
"Window of Old Rock House", 66

Cupper, Jack
"The Ruff House", 83
"The Steamboat Hotel on Main and Washington Streets", 85

Czarnowski, Norbert
"Nimitz Birthplace", 52

Eastman, Seth
"Dutch Church at Fredericksburg, Texas-70 Miles North of San Antonio, January 24, 1849", Title Page, 28
"Self Portrait", 24
"Dutch House in Fredericksburg, Texas, January 27, 1849", 25
"Dutch House in Fredericksburg, Texas, January 29, 1849", 27

Eisenlohr, Edward G.
"Church Tower", 11
Pencil drawing of "The Cross of the Pioneers" 21, 42
"Gateway and Barn at Nimitz Hotel", 40
"The Cross of the Pioneers", 41

Ethel, Lee
Drawing-Fredericksburg, 7
"Sunday Afternoon in Fredericksburg", 91

Hanna, John Austin
Drawing-Mule and Cart, 10
Sketch-Oldtimer, 16
"Mr. Dietz", 103
"A.L. Patton Building", 104

Harper, Lyne K. Lewis
Loeffler-Weber House, 55

Harvey, G.
Drawing-Mailboxes, 13
Sketch-Little Girl and Dog, 14
Sketch-Cowboy on Horseback, 17
"Texas Rancher", 99
"Round-Up", 101

Haworth, Mark
"Fredericksburg-An Enduring Heritage", Cover, Title Page 2, 3
"Cardinals", 19
"The Chicken Coop", 107
Nude Study, 109

Ingels, Elsa Muranyi
"Self Portrait", 76
"Her Wealth", 77
"Beloved" (Frank Ingels), 78

Kelly, Harold Osman (Kelly Blue)
"Fourth of July Races", 45

Klein, Irene
Distant view of Fredericksburg, 88

Lentz, Gotthold
"Main Street", 71

Lungkwitz, Hermann
"Enchanted Rock Near Fredericksburg", 31

McClusky, John D.
"Apple Tree", 20
"Cosmos", 73
Sketch-House, 75

Mintel, Edwina
Peter Tatsch Haus, 50

Muller, Virginia
"Willow City Loop", 63

Nabinger, Dollie Spidel
"Willow City Loop", 62

Petri, Friedrich Richard
"Woman and Child on Muleback and Sketches of Woman on Horse", 3
"Self Portrait", 35
"Fort Martin Scott", 37
"Campfire Scene", 38

Schiwetz, Edward Muegge (Buck)
"Fredericksburg Pioneer Museum", 59
"House on Austin Street, Fredericksburg, Texas", 60

Tarrillion, Father Peter
"St. Joseph", 34

Weber, Werner E.
"Gillespie County Courthouse", 68

Weinheimer, Felix
"St. Mary's School and Church, 1890", 48

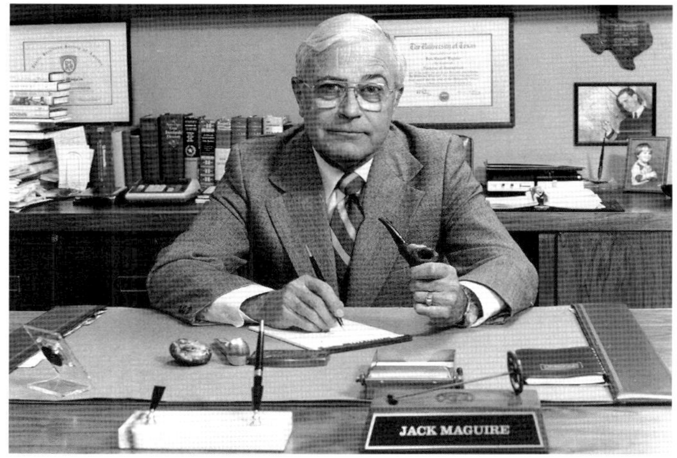

JACK MAGUIRE

When Jack Maguire appeared for a full hour on the *Larry King Show*, that famous talk show host introduced him as" Mr. Texas." King said that anybody who has written so much for so long and so successfully about the Lone Star State has to be the resident expert.

Maguire, a Fredericksburg resident, has been traveling Texas and writing about it for more than 50 years. His column, *Talk of Texas*, has been a feature in newspapers for 33 years. He has written or co-authored nine books on Texas and more than 500 articles for national magazines. He contributed to *Texas and Texans*, a history text widely adopted in the public schools. His *Texas Trivia Game* is still used as a teaching aid.

For several years, he wrote and narrated a popular radio show, *Tales of Texas*, broadcast on more than 50 stations each week. He still makes guest appearances on radio and television talk shows. Maguire has made hundreds of speeches about Texas, not only in the state but in places like New York, Washington, London, Lima, Peru, Mexico City, and Lucerne, Switzerland.

From 1976 through 1985, he was the Executive Director of the University of Texas Institute of Texan Cultures in San Antonio, a prestigious institution devoted to researching the contributions of more than 30 different ethnic and cultural groups to this state's history.

Maguire and his wife, Ann (a writer and editor in her own right), have lived in Fredericksburg for more than a decade where both continue to write about Texas.

We hope you enjoy the next 150 years in Fredericksburg as much as you enjoyed the first!